Perception and Representation
Current Issues

SECOND EDITION

Open Guides to Psychology

Series Editor: Judith Greene, Professor of Psychology
at the Open University

Perception and Representation
Current Issues
SECOND EDITION

Parts I and II
by Ilona Roth

Part III
by Vicki Bruce

Open University Press
Buckingham · Philadelphia

Open University Press
Celtic Court
22 Ballmoor
Buckingham
MK18 1XW

email: enquiries@openup.co.uk
world wide web: www.openup.co.uk

and
325 Chestnut Street
Philadelphia, PA 19106, USA

In association with The Open University

First published 1986 as *Perception and Representation: A Cognitive Approach*
Second edition first published 1995
Reprinted in this edition 1996, 1998, 2000, 2002

ISBN 0 335 19474 5

A CIP catalogue record for this book is available from the British Library

Library of Congress Cataloging-in-Publication Data

Roth, Ilona.
    Perception and representation : current issues / parts I and II by Ilona Roth, part III by Vicki Bruce. — 2nd ed.
        p.   cm.
    Includes bibliographical references and index.
    ISBN 0–335–19474–5
    1. Perception. 2. Cognition. I. Bruce, Vicki. II. Title.
BF311.R655 1995   94–41284
153.7—dc20   CIP

Edited and designed by The Open University
Typeset by Graphicraft Limited, Hong Kong
Printed in Great Britain by Biddles Limited, www.biddles.co.uk

Parts I and II of this book are dedicated to David, Benjamin, Jessica and Raphael

Perception and Representation

Contents

Part II   Object Recognition   71
Ilona Roth

Part III Perceiving and Recognizing Faces 137
Vicki Bruce

Preface

Within the Open Guides to Psychology series, *Perception and Representation* is one of a companion set of four books, the others being *Language Understanding*, *Memory* and *Problem Solving*. Together these form the main texts of the Open University third level course in Cognitive Psychology, but each of the four volumes can be read independently. The course is designed for second or third year students. It is presented in the style and format that the Open University has found to be uniquely effective in making the material intelligible and interesting.

The books provide an up-to-date and in-depth treatment of the major issues, theories and findings in cognitive psychology. They are designed to introduce a representative selection of different research methods, and the reader is encouraged, by means of Activities and Self-assessment Questions interpolated throughout the text, to become involved in cognitive psychology as an active participant.

The authors gratefully acknowledge the many helpful comments and suggestions of fellow members of the course team and of the external assessor Michael W. Eysenck on earlier drafts and the valuable assistance of Pat Vasiliou and Lynda Preston in typing the manuscript. Thanks are also due to Chris Wooldridge for his tireless work in editing the manuscript.

Acknowledgements

Grateful acknowledgement is made to John Frisby. Part II includes material based on the Part written by him for an earlier version of this book. Grateful acknowledgement is also made to the following sources for permission to reproduce material in this book:

Figures 1.2 and 1.3: Collins, A.M. and Quillian, M.R. (1969) 'Retrieval time from semantic memory', *Journal of Verbal Learning and Verbal Behaviour*, vol. 8, Academic Press Inc.; Figure 2.1: Courtesy of R.C. James; Figures 2.4 and 2.18: Mike Levers, The Open University; Figure 2.6: Josef Albers, *Steps* (circa 1931) reproduced with the permission of The Josef Albers Foundation, Inc.; Figure 2.8a: Modigliani, A. *Female Nude*, courtesy of the Courtauld Institute Galleries, London (Courtauld gift 1932); Figure 2.8b and c: Frisby, J.P. (1979) *Seeing: Illusion, Brain and Mind*, by permission of Oxford University Press; Figure 2.9: Created for this publication by Dr Mark Georgeson, Reader in the Department of Vision Sciences at the University of Aston; Figure 2.10: Marr, D. and Hildreth, E. (1980) 'Theory of edge detection', *Proc. Roy. Soc.*, B207, 187–216, figures 1 and 8. With the permission of The Royal Society, Professor Ellen C. Hildreth of Wellesley College, and of the Estate of Professor David Marr; Figures 2.11, 2.16 and 2.17: Marr, D. (1976) 'Early processing of visual information', *Phil. Trans. Roy. Soc.*, B275, 483–524, figures 4, 13 and 21. With the permission of The Royal Society and of the Estate of Professor David Marr; Figures 2.19–2.23: Marr, D. and Nishihara, H.K. (1978) 'Representation and recognition of the spatial organisation of three-dimensional shapes', *Proc. Roy. Soc.*, B200, 269–94, figures 3, 6 and 8. With the permission of The Royal Society and of the Estate of Professor David Marr, and of Dr H. Keith Nishihara of Teleos Research at Palo Alto; Figure 2.24: Based on Part A of figure 3.2 of Palmer, S.E. (1990) 'Modern theories of gestalt perception', pp. 39–70, in Humphries, G.W. (ed.) *Understanding Vision: An Interdisciplinary Perspective*, Blackwell, Oxford. With the kind permission of Blackwell Publishers and of Professor Stephen E. Palmer, University of California at Berkeley; Figures 2.25–2.29: Biederman, I. (1985) 'Computer vision', *Graphics and Image Processing*, 32, 29–73. With the permission of Academic Press and of Professor Irving Biederman, University of Southern California at Los Angeles. Our reproduction uses figures 1, 3, 12, 14 and 16 as they appear in Biederman, I. (1987) 'Recognition-by-components: a theory of human image understanding', *Psychological Review*, 94(2), 115–47; Figures 2.30 and 2.31: based on Humphreys, G.W., Riddoch, M.J. and Quinlan, P.T. (1988) 'Cascade processes in picture identification', *Cognitive Neuropsychology*, Lawrence Erlbaum Associates Ltd, reprinted by permission of Lawrence Erlbaum Associates Ltd, Hove, UK; Figure 3.1: Copyright 1987 Shaherazan; Figure 3.2: Sergent, J. (1984) 'An investigation into component and configural processes underlying face perception', *British Journal of Psychology*, 75, 221–42. With the permission of the British Psychological Society. It has not proved possible to contact Professor Justine Sergent at McGill University but we wish to acknowledge all her rights as author; Figure 3.3: Tanaka, J.W. and Farah, M.J. (1993) 'Parts and wholes in face recognition', *The Quarterly Journal of Experimental Psychology*, 46A(2), 225–46. Reprinted by permission of The Quarterly Journal of Experimental Psychology, and of Professor James Tanaka, Oberlin College, and Professor Martha Farah, University of Pennsylvania; Figure 3.4: Thompson, P. (1980) 'Margaret Thatcher: a new illusion', *Perception*, 9, 483–4. With kind permission of Pion Limited, London, and of Dr Peter Thompson, University of York; Figure 3.5: Pearson, D. et al. 'Computer generated cartoons', pages 46–60 in Barlow, H. et al. (1990) *Images and Understanding: Thoughts About Images, Ideas About Understanding*, Cambridge University Press. Reproduced with the permission of Cambridge University Press and of Professor David Pearson, University of Essex; Figure 3.6: Young, A.W., Hay, D.C. and Ellis, A.W. (1985) 'The faces that launched a thousand slips: everyday difficulties and errors in recognising people', in *British Journal of Psychology*, 76, 1985. Copyright © The British Psychological Society.

Introduction

The theme of this book is how we make sense of all the information we receive from the world via our senses. The world as we experience it is divided into relatively discrete structures. We are aware of objects and people, animals and plants, all of which have particular sizes, shapes, colours and locations. Some of these things are stationary, others move as part of complex event sequences. Each has a specific function or significance. These entities feature prominently in both our moment-to-moment perceptions of the world and the more permanent representations of the world which are stored as knowledge in memory. Each part of the book considers different aspects of how such perceptions and representations are achieved. Certain major issues re-emerge in each part.

Part I of the book is concerned with the concepts or conceptual categories which serve to organize our knowledge of the world into manageable chunks. These conceptual categories represent the shared characteristics by which individually different 'things' can be mentally grouped together and differentiated from other groupings. They are fundamental to all cognitive activity, since without them perception, memory, language and all thought processes would be impossibly un-wieldy. Much of the discussion is concerned with alternative conceptions of the nature of these mental representations. A contrast is drawn between the 'traditional' view that they are well-defined, clearly differentiated groupings of things, and the more recent idea that they are rather ill-defined, fuzzy groupings of things. One conclusion which emerges is that both these types of representation play a role in cognition. A major factor in determining the nature of concept representations is their function or purpose in cognition and communication: they may be for everyday use or for communication between experts; they may serve as stable representations of the world as we know it, or as temporary representations constructed to meet goals such as 'going on holiday'. Research which investigates how these different purposes affect the form taken by concept representations is discussed.

Relatively stable representations, for instance, in the form of stored descriptions of what chairs, tables, birds and plants typically look like, are necessary if we are actually to see and recognize these objects. Part II seeks to explain how the information received by the visual sense organs is processed and compared with these stored representations in order to yield 'interpretations' of what objects are, what are their functions or meanings, and what they are called. Much of the discussion is concerned with the nature of the processes which lead, ultimately, to this recognition. However, the nature of the stored representations is necessarily a continuing theme in this part.

A general explanatory assumption adopted in this second part is that the perceptual processes leading to object recognition consist of a series of identifiable stages. One of the goals of the discussion is to consider what these stages are, in what order they occur, and whether they interact with each other.

Part II also illustrates a variety of methods for studying object recognition, including simple demonstrations of visual phenomena, experiments, neuropsychological studies of visual deficits following brain damage, and artificial intelligence approaches in which a computer is programmed to 'see' or 'recognize' objects. The discussion shows that no-one has yet designed an artificial system which matches the apparently effortless way in which we see, recognize and interact with the complex world around us.

Among our most complex interactions are those with other human beings. Fundamental to these interactions is our ability to recognize the faces of people we know. The processes and representations responsible for our remarkable skill in this area form the topic of Part III of this volume. An important theme running through this third part is the extent to which the processes and representations for face recognition are the same as those for recognizing objects, and the extent to which face recognition is 'special'.

Besides considering how we decide that a face is familiar (face recognition *per se*), Part III considers the way in which facial expressions and facial speech are recognized. The important contribution of neuropsychological work is well illustrated in this area of discussion: the fact that patients with brain damage may display selective loss of the ability to recognize faces while retaining the ability to recognize expressions or facial speech argues for independent processing of the respective sources of information.

Finally, this third part considers some different models proposed to account for person recognition. In considering these, the reader will be able to draw upon basic concepts developed in Part II, concerning the nature of processing stages and how they are organized with respect to one another.

How to use this guide

In this book the reader will find activities and Self-Assessment Questions (SAQs) inserted at various points in the text. Doing the Activities will give a deeper insight into, and a better understanding of, some of the phenomena described and the research techniques used to investigate them. The SAQs provide the reader with a means of checking his or her understanding. The answers can be found at the end of the book and will help to illuminate points made in the text. Doing the Activities and answering the SAQs engages the reader as an active participant rather than just a passive recipient. He or she is induced to carry out the more active processing which is known to produce better comprehension and retention of what is read.

Detailed accounts of empirical investigations are presented in Techniques Boxes and these are chosen as illustrative of representative empirical methods. The Summaries recapitulate the main points in each section and provide a useful aid to revision. The Index of Concepts that appears at the end of the book allows the reader to locate the place in the text where important concepts are first introduced and defined. Entries in the index of concepts are in bold in the text. Also at the end of the book is an Overview which considers some of the main themes which run through all three parts.

Each part concludes with a short list of recommended further reading. Obviously, the interested reader can also follow up the references given in the text. In addition, he or she may like to look at the other Cognitive Psychology volumes in the Open Guides to Psychology series and at *Cognitive Psychology: A Student's Handbook* by Eysenck and Keane which is the set book for the Open University course in Cognitive Psychology.

Part I
Conceptual Categories

Ilona Roth

Contents

1   *Introduction*

One of the most important characteristics of cognition is that objects, entities and events, though individually different, are treated in thought and language as members of **conceptual categories**. The concept 'chair', for instance, is a mental grouping of objects which are individually different, but which tend to share certain characteristics in common. The same is true of entities such as 'shopping list' and events such as 'birthday party'. **Concepts** or conceptual categories, then, are **mental representations** of objects, entities or events stored in memory.

In the ensuing discussion, the terms 'concept' and 'conceptual category' will be used interchangeably to refer to mental representations of objects, entities and events. The term **categorization** will be used to describe the mental activity of grouping like things together into conceptual categories. Two other terms — **class** and **classification** — are roughly synonymous with 'conceptual category' and 'categorization'.

There is a particularly close and intricate connection between concepts and the words used to express them. For instance, 'chair' is both a concept and a word in our language — so can the two really be distinguished? As a rule of thumb, the concept 'chair' is an abstract representation of the class of objects in question, stored in memory. In contrast, the word 'chair' is what we utter or write when referring to this class of objects. Observation of organisms having no language (e.g. pigeons or young children) suggests that they can respond systematically to classes of objects, such as shapes of a particular colour, or foods with a particular taste. It seems that they are able to form abstract representations or concepts of these classes, even though they cannot talk about them. On the other hand, the fact that an adult uses the word 'chair' correctly is one of the ways we know he or she possesses the concept of a chair. It follows that the relationship between conceptual categorization and language is a complex one. It has generated a great deal of empirical research but this is beyond the scope of the present discussion.

1.1   *The importance of concepts*

Why is the ability to categorize or form concepts such an integral and central part of cognition? Try to imagine a world in which we did not treat objects such as chairs as members of conceptual categories. One problem is that each object which we in fact perceive or 'see as' a chair would be seen as a novel object — we would be unable to *recognize* or *make sense* of such perceptions because we would have no common label to attach to them. Thus, the ability to place objects in conceptual categories is a fundamental property of *perception*.

19

A second difficulty is that we would not know what to do with any new 'chair' we encountered — for example, that it could be sat on. We understand about the function of chairs because this is part of the conceptual knowledge we have of that class of objects. Without this knowledge we would be unable to use or interact appropriately with 'chairs'. It can be concluded that the ability to categorize is essential for *action* — our responses to and interactions with the objects, entities and events which make up our world.

Memory, too, would function inefficiently without the ability to organize the knowledge we acquire into meaningful categories. We would be forced to store trivial information, such as the details of each chair we had come across, instead of retaining only essential information, such as the characteristics of chairs in general and relevant knowledge about personally important chairs (my own armchair, the baby's high chair).

Finally, without conceptual categories, it would be extremely difficult to *communicate* about objects such as chairs. If we wanted to tell someone that we had just seen a chair, we would have to describe laboriously all the individual parts of the object, rather than simply denoting them by the single world 'chair'. Communication would become totally unwieldy. In short, conceptual categorization is central to all our cognitive abilities. As some writers have aptly put it: 'Concepts are the coinage of thought' (Johnson-Laird and Wason, 1977, p.169).

A general principle underlying all these functions of categorization is that of **cognitive economy**. Categories serve to minimize cognitive effort by representing aspects of our world in the most informative but economical way. For instance, we do not (generally speaking) treat chairs made of wood, metal and plastic as separate categories, because these distinctions are not very useful in recognizing, thinking about, and discussing chairs. On the other hand, it *is* useful to distinguish between chairs and tables because there is an important difference in their function — chairs are for sitting on, tables are for putting things on.

1.2   Research on concepts

Part I will consider psychological research on concepts. Research in this area falls under three main headings. First, there is the question of how concepts are mentally represented. This research is concerned with the content and structure of people's **representations** for categories such as 'chair'. Are such concepts characterized by hard and fast rules (e.g. all chairs have four legs) or rules of thumb (e.g. chairs usually have four legs)? Do lists of properties (legs, arms, backrest, etc.) play a role in representation?

A second area of research is concerned with how we decide to what category a particular item belongs. Given that we have concepts such as 'chair', 'bench' and 'stool' represented in memory, how do we decide on the appropriate categorization for a new object we encounter. This question concerns the **processes** by which particular objects, entities or events are assigned to appropriate categories.

Finally, there is the question of how conceptual categories are acquired in the first place. For instance, how do we acquire the knowledge that enables us to classify and respond to objects such as chairs appropriately? In part this is a question about the cognitive development of children. Most of us have observed the gradual process by which children come to use terms such as 'chair' appropriately. Initially, a child may use the term for several items of furniture and only gradually narrow it down to apply to that group of objects which we, as adults, classify as chairs. But **concept acquisition** is not only a phenomenon of childhood — it continues throughout adult life. Think of the *new* concepts which we acquire as we get older: they range from concrete concepts, such as the parts of a car or the ingredients of a dish, to highly abstract concepts, such as socialism or fashion. So concept acquisition is a central facet of both child development and adult cognition. Research on this topic is concerned with the strategies used in acquiring new concepts.

To summarize, an understanding of how we categorize focuses upon three main issues:

1 Representations: how are conceptual categories mentally represented?
2 Processes: how are particular items assigned to these categories?
3 Acquisition: how are these categories acquired?

The present chapter will be mainly concerned with concept representation, though the discussion will inevitably touch upon the processes by which items are assigned to conceptual categories and the acquisition of new categories. Experimental studies often employ categorization or acquisition tasks as a way of tapping subjects' mental representations. One area which will not be covered is concept acquisition in children. The further reading section at the end of this chapter lists some references you could follow up.

Summary of Section 1

- A concept or conceptual category is a mental representation of a set of objects, events or entities.
- Concepts may be distinguished from the words which express them, though there is a close connection between the two.
- The ability to group individually different items into conceptual

categories according to their shared characteristics is central to all cognitive activities, including perception, planning of action, memory and communication.

- Conceptual categories serve to represent objects, events and entities with maximum information and minimum cognitive effort. This is known as the principle of cognitive economy.
- The study of conceptual categorization is concerned with three main questions:
  How are conceptual categories mentally represented?
  By what processes are particular items assigned to these categories?
  By what strategies are these categories acquired?

2   The defining feature approach

Earlier work on concept representation was dominated by one idea: that individual concepts are represented by lists of properties or features which serve to *define* these concepts. This notion, which originates from the Greek philosopher Aristotle, is known as the **defining feature approach**. In order to understand the main assumptions of the approach, let us consider, using our own introspections as the basis, the way in which people represent a geometric concept such as 'triangle'. This technique is sometimes known as a **thought experiment**.

2.1   Defining features for a geometric concept

Imagine that you are asked to explain what is meant by a concept such as 'triangle' to someone who is unfamiliar with this type of figure. You would try to give a description of the shared identifying characteristics of triangles by which the person might recognize one.

Activity 1
Using the guidelines just given, write down a description which characterizes the conceptual category 'triangle'. Cover up the remainder of the page while you write down your answer.

My answer looks like this:
(a) Two-dimensional geometric figure.
(b) Has three straight sides.
(c) Sides are joined to each other at their ends.
(d) Has angles adding up to 180°.

In my list for 'triangle', each item refers to a **property** associated with triangles. You will come across this term frequently in the forthcoming discussion, along with the term **feature**. The two terms are more or less interchangeable, though the term 'feature' is used particularly for those properties which are perceptual. For instance, items (b) 'has three straight sides' and (c) 'sides are joined to each other at their ends' are **perceptual properties** — what we can tell about triangles by looking at them. For other categories we might list properties which are auditory, tactile, olfactory, etc. Item (d) 'angles add up to 180°' is also a property of triangles, but it is not perceptual — it is not something we could discover about triangles by looking at them. Instead, it is a mathematical or **formal property**.

The most important point is that items (a), (b), (c) and (d) are properties of *all* triangles. These properties are described as **necessary properties** of triangles, because a figure cannot be a triangle unless it possesses them. However, of these four properties, only (b) and (d) apply just to triangles. Item (a) and item (c) are also properties of geometric figures such as quadrilaterals, pentagons, etc. If we want to describe triangles in a way which distinguishes them from these other figures, we must use all four properties in combination: 'two-dimensional geometric figure, having three straight sides, joined at their ends, and angles adding up to 180°.' This is a description which applies to all triangles and only triangles. It is said to be both **necessary and sufficient** for the category 'triangle', because any figure which possesses this combination of properties is guaranteed to be a triangle whereas any figure which does not possess the combination of properties cannot be a triangle. The description serves as a **definition** of the category 'triangle' which clearly distinguishes it from other categories such as squares and rectangles, shoes and sausages!

SAQ 1
(a) The following list of properties is *necessary* for the category 'square', but it is not *sufficient*. Why?
   Two-dimensional geometric figure.
   Has four straight sides.
   Sides are joined at their ends.
   Angles add up to 360°.

(b) Which two properties, if added, would convert the description into a set of necessary and sufficient properties which define the category 'square'?

It should be clear that it is possible to specify geometric concepts such as 'triangle' or 'square' in terms of a combination of defining properties which apply (equally) to all category members. But this is an **external specification** (i.e. one which is formulated overtly, outside our heads). The fact that we can 'externally' specify geometric figures in this way does not necessarily imply that the mental representations stored in human memory also take this form, but it makes it in principle possible. The core assumption of the defining feature approach is that mental representations of concepts *do* in fact take this form; that is:

- **Concepts are mentally represented as combinations of necessary and sufficient properties which define the categories so represented.**

Several further assumptions, listed below, follow from this main assumption:

- **The representation of a category will apply equally and to the same extent to all category members.**
  What this means is that all figures to which the definition applies are equally 'good' triangles — the definition cannot apply more to some triangles than to others. There is no such thing as a 'borderline' case — a figure which is like a triangle, but not clearly a member of the category.
- **All concepts are represented in this way (i.e. not just geometric concepts, but everyday concepts such as 'chair', biological concepts such as 'horse', and so on).**
- **All people represent concepts (triangle, chair, etc.) in the same way (i.e. as combinations of necessary and sufficient conditions constituting definitions).**

The defining feature approach makes a further assumption about how the relationship between concepts in the same domain (e.g. triangle, quadrilateral, pentagon, etc.) is mentally represented. To introduce this assumption, let's return to the example of a geometric concept.

2.2   Hierarchical organization of a geometric concept

Among the individual properties for 'triangle' listed in response to Activity 1, item (a) 'two-dimensional geometric figure' shows that we may think of the category 'triangle' as belonging to a more general category, along with other categories such as 'quadrilateral' and 'pentagon'. Thus, geometric figures (triangle, quadrilateral, pentagon) are thought of as belonging to a common **superordinate** category. We may also differentiate each of these individual categories into smaller groupings — for triangle, these would be 'equilateral', 'isosceles', etc. These are **subordinate** categories of the concept 'triangle'. All this information may be represented in the form of a diagram (see Figure 1.1).

Figure 1.1 is a way of organizing information known as a **hierarchy**. The main principle of hierarchical organization is that a general or most inclusive category (the superordinate) appears at the top of the hierarchy. This superordinate category includes or subsumes more

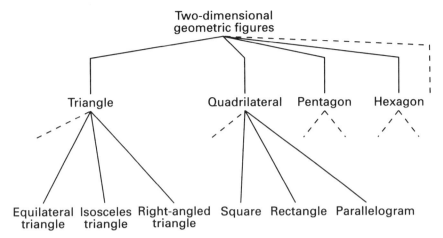

Figure 1.1 A hierarchical organization for two-dimensional geometric figures. Dotted lines indicate other sub-categories not specified in the diagram

specific categories which appear at the next level down. This is the intermediate level in Figure 1.1. Further down again are even more specific categories which are included within each of the intermediate level categories. These are the subordinate categories. The hierarchy thus shows all the relationships between categories in a particular domain, in this case two-dimensional geometric figures. In this example, the hierarchy has just three levels, but other kinds of categories may lend themselves to more complex hierarchies having many more levels. Notice that categories at levels below the superordinate category have a dual function: as **members** of their parent category and as categories in their own right. In their function as category members they are also referred to as **instances** or **exemplars**. You will come across these terms frequently in later discussion.

2.3 *Inheritance of properties in conceptual hierarchies*

Suppose that we now add into the hierarchy the properties which apply to the conceptual categories at each of the levels. The superordinate category is defined by the single property 'two-dimensional geometric figure'.

Now if you work out what properties are appropriate to each of the categories at the next level down, you will see that they **inherit** the properties of the superordinate concept, but also acquire additional properties which serve to distinguish them from the superordinate category and from each other.

Thus, 'triangle' inherits the property 'two-dimensional geometric figure', but in addition acquires the properties:

Has three straight sides.

Sides are joined to each other at the ends.

Has angles adding up to 180°.

The same phenomenon is repeated at the subordinate level. Thus, 'equilateral triangle' inherits all properties of the 'triangle', but in addition acquires the property:

Sides are equal in length.

We thus have a strict pattern of inheritance, in which a concept at a given level is defined by combining the defining properties of its 'parent' concept with further defining properties specific to this level.

According to the defining feature approach, this pattern is characteristic of the way concepts are mentally represented. So the final assumption of the defining feature approach is that:

- **A concept at a given level in a hierarchy is represented by a combination of the inherited properties which define the parent concept together with further defining properties.**

One attempt to test these assumptions of the defining feature approach was made in a now classic study by Collins and Quillian (1969). They proposed that people's internal, mentally stored representations of biological classes take the form of a hierarchy; that individual concepts within the hierarchy are represented by definitions; and that the defining properties of general concepts are inherited by their more specific subordinates.

2.4   Collins and Quillian's conceptual hierarchy

Figure 1.2 shows part of Collins and Quillian's version of a zoological hierarchy. At the top of the hierarchy are **nodes** corresponding to broad general categories, or superordinates, in this case *animal*. These break down into more specific categories such as *mammal, bird, fish*. These in turn break down into even more specific categories (e.g. *canary, ostrich*). At each level in the hierarchy, the category nodes are linked to a list of defining properties such as 'eats' or 'has feathers'. The more general superordinate categories are linked to a list of general defining properties which are shared by all category members. These properties are inherited by all the subordinate categories, though they are not actually listed at subordinate levels. Only the additional properties, not applicable at the level above, are actually listed. For instance, the representation for the category 'bird' consists of features such as 'has wings', 'can fly', which are assumed to apply to all birds. These properties are inherited at the next level down (e.g. canary), but only the specific additional properties ('can sing', 'is yellow') are listed. This is an elegant way of achieving 'cognitive economy' (see Section 1.1), since it means that a property such as 'can fly' is only listed once — for birds — and not for each individual type of bird. Notice that the model employs a special type of defining property for cases such as 'ostrich', which represents an exception to the general defining rule that birds can fly. In order to reflect this exception, the inheritance of the property 'can fly' is cancelled by listing, with ostrich, the property 'can't fly'.

In order to test the assumptions of the model, Collins and Quillian specified mental processes by which information can be retrieved from the hierarchy. Suppose that someone is trying to work out whether a statement such as 'A canary is an animal' is true. In order to verify this statement, the person must locate the relevant category (i.e. the 'animal' node) and decide whether canary is a member of it. As Figure 1.2 shows, this requires a search through two levels in the hierarchy. On the other hand, if the statement to be verified is 'A canary is a bird', there is only one level between the two category nodes. Collins and Quillian argued that, since subjects need time to search through the hierarchy, the first statement should take longer to verify than the second. Similarly, if subjects are asked to verify property statements such as 'A canary can breathe' (two-level search), this should take longer than 'A canary has wings' (one-level search). Finally, in general these property statements should take longer to verify than 'category'

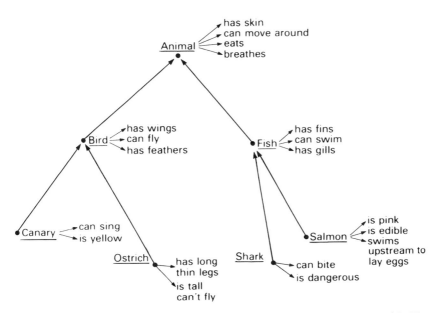

Figure 1.2   Part of Collins and Quillian's hierarchy for animals   (Collins and Quillian, 1969, Figure 1)

statements, since the subject must retrieve a property ('has wings') as well as locating the category which possesses this property. In order to test their model, Collins and Quillian used a task known as **sentence verification**, as shown in Techniques Box A.

This study provided general support for the idea that the conceptual categories in a given domain are represented hierarchically. However, subsequent work showed that the model was incorrect in some important details. For one thing, it was found that sentences such as 'A dog

---

TECHNIQUES BOX A

Sentence Verification Experiments (Collins and Quillian, 1969)

Rationale

To investigate the times taken to verify statements about animals. If categories are organized hierarchically, it should take longer to deal with sentences involving category information from non-adjacent levels. In addition, if categories are represented as nodes linked to defining properties, statements about properties of animals should take longer to verify than statements about category membership.

Method

Subjects were asked to decide whether presented sentences are true or false. Sentences involved either no-level, one-level or two-level searches, and could be of two main types: *category verification* or *property verification* (see Table 1.1).

Table 1.1

Category verification	Property verification	No. of levels
A canary is a canary	A canary can sing	0
A canary is a bird	A canary can fly	1
A canary is an animal	A canary has skin	2
A canary is a fish	A canary has gills	False

Sentences like these were displayed one at a time on a screen and reaction times were measured between the onset of the sentence and the subject pressing a 'true' or 'false' button.

Results

Figure 1.3 shows that the mean times taken by subjects to verify sentences (vertical axis) depended on the number of levels which must be searched (horizontal axis). In addition, the 'property' sentences took longer than the 'category' sentences. This is consistent with the hierarchical model proposed by Collins and Quillian.

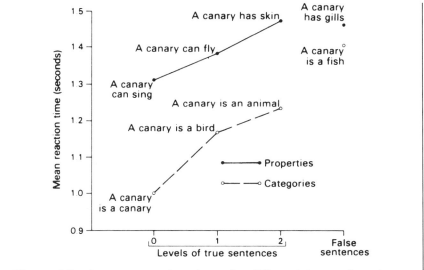

Figure 1.3   Average reaction times for different types of sentence (Collins and Quillian, 1969, Figure 2)

is a mammal' took longer to verify than 'A dog is an animal'. Yet according to the hierarchy adopted by Collins and Quillian, the second sentence requires a search through more levels than the first. A possible reason for this is that 'mammal' is a relatively unfamiliar category for many subjects, and therefore not clearly or correctly represented in their personal hierarchy for animals. In a study of people's knowledge of zoological classification, I asked people to draw up their own hierarchies using zoological terms taken from different levels in the scientific hierarchy or **taxonomy**. Some people were uncertain or mistaken about the correct location of terms such as 'mammal' within the animal kingdom, and this was related to how much they knew about zoology. Collins and Quillian's model failed to allow for differences in *knowledge*, which might result in variations in the hierarchical structures used by different people to represent animal categories. Indeed, the zoological hierarchy which Collins and Quillian adopted in their model was only their own much simplified version of the scientific taxonomy used by zoologists.

A further problem was that certain pairs of sentences yielded different verification times even though both involved a search through the same number of levels. For instance, a sentence such as 'A robin is a bird' was more rapidly verified than 'A parrot is a bird', suggesting that the two instances 'robin' and 'parrot' do not have the same status within the category 'bird'.

29

SAQ 2
Look back at the assumptions of the defining feature approach listed on pages 24 and 26. Which of these are questioned and which supported by Collins and Quillian's study and the subsequent findings described above?

To conclude, Collins and Quillian's claim that individual categories are related to one another within hierarchies has been upheld in later research. However, the specific assumptions of the defining feature approach which they built around this general claim are contradicted by the evidence. In the next section we shall consider experimental tasks which suggest a reason why items such as 'robin' and 'parrot' have different status within the category 'bird'. Subjects in such experiments think of 'robin' as a more typical instance of 'bird' than 'parrot'. This single insight has most influenced psychologists to rethink the defining feature view of representation.

Summary of Section 2

- A geometric category such as triangle lends itself to external specification in terms of a combination of necessary and sufficient properties which clearly defines the category and distinguishes it from other categories.
- The defining feature approach assumes that concepts are mentally represented in this way.
- From this follow the further assumptions that the definition of a concept applies equally and to the same extent to all its exemplars; that all concepts are so represented; and that all people represent concepts in the same way.
- According to the defining feature approach, when related concepts are represented as a hierarchy, concepts at a given level inherit the defining properties of the parent concept and acquire additional defining properties which distinguish them from the parent concept and from other concepts at the same level.
- Collins and Quillian (1969) proposed a model for hierarchical representation of biological concepts based on these assumptions. Sentence verification studies supported the general notion of conceptual hierarchies but indicated, contrary to the defining feature view, that people's knowledge of categories, and the varying typicality of category members must be taken into account.

3   Rosch's fuzzy concept approach

Much of the theoretical and empirical work which casts doubt on the defining feature approach has its origins in work by Rosch (1973, 1975). In this section we will consider some representative experiments as well as the general theoretical approach, often known as the **fuzzy concept approach**, which Rosch proposed as an alternative to the defining feature approach.

In Section 2 we considered 'triangle' as a type of category which can be externally specified in terms of defining properties, perhaps implying that its mental representation also takes this form. Rosch's studies employed so-called 'everyday' categories, a term which covers manufactured objects (artefacts) such as furniture, toys and clothing; everyday activities such as sports; and biological categories such as birds, fruit and vegetables. Some of these categories — particularly the artefacts — are difficult to specify, externally, in terms of defining properties, as we shall see in Activity 2.

3.1   An everyday concept

Activity 2
Just as for Activity 1, see if you can write down a description which characterizes the category 'chair'. Cover up the rest of the page while you write your answer.

Your answer probably looks something like this:
(a) Furniture.
(b) Used for sitting on.
(c) Has flat horizontal surface.
(d) Usually has four legs.
(e) Usually has a straight backrest.
(f) May have arms.

In some ways this list resembles the one drawn up for 'triangle'. Item (a) provides a superordinate category which includes chair, table, desk and other categories of furniture. And since chair can be divided into subordinate categories such as kitchen chair, dining chair, etc., information about chairs, like triangles, can be represented as a hierarchy. Items (c), (d), (e) and (f) give perceptual features of chairs. Item (b), like (d) in the 'triangle' list, is a non-perceptual property. In this case, the property concerns the function of chairs. **Functional properties** seem to play an important part in specifying many categories of everyday objects.

Following the same procedure adopted for the category 'triangle', we can ask which if any of the properties are necessary?

SAQ 3
Identify any properties in the list which an object must have to be a chair (i.e. necessary properties).

The striking contrast between this list and the one for triangle is that, while there are two (non-perceptual) properties which are necessary for chairs, there are also several perceptual features which, though often associated with chairs, are not truly necessary. For instance, though *many* chairs have a flat horizontal surface for sitting on, some have a sloping surface, some have a curved surface. Similarly, many chairs have four legs, but there are also chairs with three, one or even no legs.

Figure 1.4
What is a chair?
Each of these chairs
has a different set of
properties

Similar exceptions can be found for items (e) and (f). Figure 1.4 shows just a few of the many objects which count as chairs. They are all clearly recognizable as chairs, and yet each of them is an exception to at least one of the properties on our list.

A further contrast between this and our 'triangle' list is that there is no combination of properties which appears to refer to all chairs and only chairs (i.e. a combination of necessary and sufficient properties constituting a definition). Thus, items (a) and (b) are necessary for chairs, but they also apply to seats, benches and stools, so they are not sufficient to allow categorization of an object as a chair. Even when we add properties (c), (d), (e) and (f), we still do not have a description which applies only to chairs.

SAQ 4
Why is the combination of properties (a) to (f) not sufficient to guarantee that an object is a chair?

You may find yourself disagreeing with some of my claims about the properties of chairs — but this is significant in itself! Whereas there seems little room for argument about what defines a triangle, it seems difficult to specify any combination of properties which will be generally agreed to constitute a definition of 'chair'. Only the superordinate category (furniture) and the function (for sitting on) clearly apply to all chairs, but these properties also apply to several other categories. It seems then that chairs, unlike triangles, cannot be externally specified in terms of defining properties which apply to all chairs and only to chairs. This does not preclude the possibility that the mental representation for 'chair' takes the form of a definition, but it makes it less likely.

An alternative type of representation is suggested by the perceptual properties which I have listed for chairs. Notice that (c), (d) and (e) are all features that we might associate with a *typical* chair. Hence we might think of chairs as typically having four legs, a flat horizontal surface, and a straight backrest, even though we know of exceptions. This suggests that our mental representation for objects such as a chair may be based upon the characteristics of typical members of the class. Obviously, this mental representation will not apply equally or fully to all members of the class. There will be some objects (the atypical ones) which share very little in common with the mental representation. In fact, they may be so unlike a typical chair that it is unclear whether they belong to the category or not. Look, for instance, at the example in Figure 1.5 overleaf.

We shall now consider empirical evidence which suggests that **typicality** is central to the way we represent everyday categories.

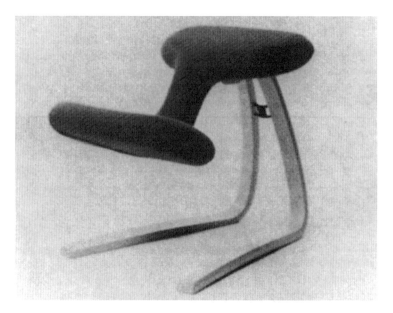

Figure 1.5   An atypical chair, known as a 'Balans' chair

3.2 Typicality effects

In a whole series of experiments, Rosch and others have shown that many categories of everyday objects appear to have **internal structure**: that is, the exemplars of a category such as furniture are not thought of as being equal in status: some exemplars (e.g. chair) are thought of as more typical than others (e.g. wardrobe). One such study is described in Techniques Box B. This is a rather different way of investigating people's category representations than the listing of properties you did in Activities 1 and 2. The aim of the study is to reveal how people represent concepts at the superordinate level (i.e. the category 'furniture' rather than the category 'chair'). The subjects' task, known as **typicality rating**, is to rate the category members (chair, table, etc.) according to how well they represent their parent category.

TECHNIQUES BOX B

Studies of Typicality Ratings (Rosch 1973, 1975)

Rationale
To investigate whether some members of conceptual categories are thought of as 'better' or more typical exemplars than others.

Method

Subjects were presented with the names of familiar superordinate categories, each followed by a randomly ordered list of category members (e.g. Superordinate: furniture. Category members: table, bed, desk, rocking chair, etc.). The superordinate categories used for the task were: furniture, vehicle, weapon, carpenter's tool, toy, sport, clothing, fruit, vegetable, bird.

For each superordinate category, subjects were asked to rate each category member according to how good an example it is of the category. Here is an extract from Rosch's instructions:

> You are to rate how good an example of the category each member is on a 7-point scale. A '1' means that you feel the member is a very good example of your idea of what the category is. A '7' means you feel the member fits very poorly with your idea or image of the category (or is not a member at all). A '4' means you feel the member fits moderately well. For example, one of the members of the category *fruit* is apple. If apple fits well with your idea of fruit put a 1 after it; if apple fits your idea of fruit very poorly you would put a 7 after it; a 4 would indicate moderate fit. Use the other numbers of the 7-point scale to indicate intermediate judgement.   (Rosch, 1975, p.198)

Large numbers of subjects were used for such studies in order to provide *normative* data; that is, data which would be representative of the behaviour of a whole population.

Results

1 In Rosch's studies, subjects reported that they found the task simple and that it seemed quite natural to think of category items as differing in how well they exemplify the category.

2 There was a high level of agreement between ratings given by different subjects (i.e. if one subject rated a particular item as a good example, other subjects were likely to do the same).

3 Further studies suggested that the ratings subjects produce in these tasks are little affected by familiarity or frequency of the category words being rated (i.e. subjects rate 'table' as a good example of furniture because they think of it as typical, *not* because the word 'table' is more familiar than other words such as 'bureau').

Table 1.2 overleaf shows the 12 items of furniture given the highest mean ratings in Rosch's study, and the 12 items of furniture given the lowest mean ratings. Altogether, subjects rated 60 items of furniture, and the items in Table 1.2 are shown rank ordered according to the mean rating given by subjects.

Conclusion
Subjects think of some category members as better examples (more typical members) than others.

Table 1.2 Norms for goodness-of-example ratings for 'furniture' (from Rosch, 1975, Table A1)

Twelve items with highest typicality ratings			Twelve items with lowest typicality ratings		
Item	Rank order	Mean typicality rating	Item	Rank order	Mean typicality rating
chair	1.5	1.04	sewing machine	49	5.39
sofa	1.5	1.04	stove	50	5.40
couch	3.5	1.10	counter	51	5.44
table	3.5	1.10	clock	52	5.48
easy chair	5	1.33	drapes	53	5.67
dresser	6.5	1.37	refrigerator	54	5.70
rocking chair	6.5	1.37	picture	55	5.75
coffee table	8	1.38	closet	56	5.95
rocker	9	1.42	vase	57	6.23
love seat	10	1.44	ashtray	58	6.35
chest of drawers	11	1.48	fan	59	6.49
desk	12	1.54	telephone	60	6.68

SAQ 5
Below is a list of items taken from the category 'vegetable':
mushroom   lettuce   sweetcorn   artichoke
pumpkin   parsnip   pea   rice
leek   radish

Use the rating scale explained in Techniques Box B to rate each item from 1 to 7 according to how well you think it exemplifies the category. It does not matter if you give the same rating to more than one item. Once you have given each item a rating, arrange the list of items in order, from the one(s) you have given the highest typicality rating to the one(s) you have given the lowest. Now compare your order with the one given in the SAQ answer. If your order is different from the one in the SAQ answer, which is based on Rosch's American subjects, can you think of a reason?

From the findings discussed in Techniques Box B, Rosch concluded that typicality is fundamental to the way people mentally represent conceptual categories. She proposed that members of a category are mentally 'ordered' according to their typicality. Metaphorically, the most typical members are at the 'centre' of the category and the least typical members at the 'edge' with a dimension of typicality between the two.

But just how fundamental is typicality? It could be argued that while people produce typicality ratings in experiments, they do not mentally represent categories in this way. This is a special case of the problem, already touched on, of assuming a direct correspondence between people's external behaviour and characteristics of their mental representations. Experimental subjects may be responding to what they perceive as the **demand characteristics** of the experiment (i.e. what they think the experimenter requires of them, rather than giving responses which reflect their normal thought processes). Though Rosch emphasized that her subjects considered the task natural, these introspective reports cannot be counted as strong evidence that their external responses reflect their mental representations. Even the high level of agreement between subjects' ratings is inconclusive. Perhaps large numbers of subjects were merely tackling the experimental task in the same way.

More persuasive is the fact that typicality affects people's performance in various cognitive tasks where demand characteristics are less likely to operate. We have already touched on the effects of typicality on reaction times (RTs), which posed difficulties for Collins and Quillian's study (see Techniques Box A). Techniques Box C describes a study specifically designed to investigate the effects of typicality on the times taken to decide whether category items belong to particular superordinate categories.

TECHNIQUES BOX C

The Effects of Typicality on Categorization of Concept Words
(Rosch, 1973)

Rationale
To investigate whether the typicality of a category word affects the time taken to decide if it is a member of a superordinate category. If people represent categories in terms of typicality, category judgements should be faster for typical items.

Method
On each trial, subjects were given the name of a *target concept* such as 'bird' followed by a *test item* such as 'robin'. Subjects had to decide as quickly as possible whether or not the test item was a member of the target category. See Table 1.3 for examples.

Table 1.3

Trial	Target concept	Test item	Correct response
1	Furniture	Chair	Yes
2	Vegetable	Table	No
3	Furniture	Clock	Yes
4	Vegetable	Radish	Yes
5	Vegetable	Mushroom	Yes

Results
1 The times for 'yes' responses were affected by typicality — the more typical the test item (as judged from typicality ratings produced as in Techniques Box B), the faster the time taken to decide that it was a member of the target category.
2 Error rates were affected by typicality — there were fewer errors in categorizing more typical words.

SAQ 6
Comparing Table 1.3 with Table 1.2 and the answer to SAQ 5, work out which of the items in the following pairs should be categorized faster:
    Chair or clock
    Radish or mushroom

The basic finding that typicality can affect the speed with which category membership is judged has been replicated many times. Other studies (e.g. Mervis et al., 1976) indicate that typicality can affect the order in which category items are remembered. For instance, when subjects are asked to list all the members of a given category they tend to produce items in order of their typicality. Similarly, studies of the acquisition of categories by children suggest that they tend to learn typical members of a category before atypical members (Mervis, 1980). In short, typicality affects people's performance in a wide variety of cognitive tasks where demand characteristics are less likely to be responsible for the pattern of results.

3.3 Fuzzy boundaries

Further empirical evidence against the defining feature approach described in Section 2 comes from studies of the boundaries of categories. According to the defining feature approach, these boundaries should be clear-cut and stable. For example, there should be no difficulty in deciding whether a given item of furniture is a chair or a stool, and no change in the way it is categorized depending on context. But, as we saw in Activity 2, these assumptions are questionable. Empirical evidence that the boundaries of certain categories are fuzzy and dependent on **context** comes from a study by Labov (1973), described in Techniques Box D.

TECHNIQUES BOX D

The Effect of Context on Categorization of Objects (Labov, 1973)

Rationale
To investigate whether people categorize pictures of objects differently depending on the context. If so, this implies that the category boundaries are not clear-cut and stable.

Method
In Labov's study, subjects were shown a series of twenty drawings of objects resembling household receptacles, and asked to name the objects depicted. Figure 1.6 shows the first four drawings: the first drawing bears a strong resemblance to a cup, and the other three drawings are progressively less cup-like. The remaining sixteen objects were drawn to look less and less like cups.

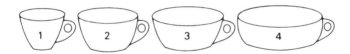

Figure 1.6   The first four drawings used by Labov

Four subject groups were supplied with one of four different contextual cues to be used in naming the objects:

Subject group	Condition	Instruction
A	Neutral	Imagine the object held in someone's hand.
B	Coffee	Imagine someone holding the object and drinking coffee from it.
C	Food	Imagine the object filled with mashed potatoes and sitting on the dinner table.
D	Flower	Imagine the object on a shelf filled with cut flowers.

Results

The results clearly showed that *context* had an effect on how subjects classified the object. For instance, for drawing number one, all subjects in the 'neutral' and 'coffee' conditions, and most subjects in the 'food' and 'flower' conditions, gave the response 'cup'. By the third drawing, subjects in the 'neutral' and 'coffee' conditions were no longer consistently calling the object a cup, and the percentage of 'cup' responses for 'food' and 'flower' subjects was very low indeed — these subjects tended to give the response 'bowl' and 'vase' respectively. By the twentieth drawing, the percentage of 'cup' responses by subjects in the 'food' and 'flower' conditions had fallen to zero, whereas the percentages for the 'neutral' and 'coffee' condition were still at about 10 per cent and 15 per cent respectively. These results suggest that subjects can define the boundary of a category such as 'cup' differently depending on the contextual condition — that is, the boundary is flexible rather than fixed. Also, as there was no abrupt decline in the number of 'cup' responses from one drawing to the next, but a gradual transition from this response to others, the boundary of the category appears to be fuzzy rather than clear-cut.

These results cast doubt on the defining feature approach. Notice, however, that the stimulus material in Labov's study consisted of simple drawings. It could be argued that such materials play down the distinctiveness of *real* cups and thus exaggerate the overlap between this and other types of household receptacles.

3.4 Rosch's prototype

So far, we have considered three lines of evidence which conflict with the predictions of the defining feature approach. First, Activity 2, though not a formal experiment, implied that people have difficulty generating defining properties for an everyday category like 'chair'. This suggests that, even if people represent mathematical categories such as 'triangle' in terms of definitions, they do not do so for everyday categories. Secondly, Rosch's typicality studies showed that people do not think of the members of everyday categories as equally good examples: some are thought of as highly typical, while others are thought of as atypical, and this affects how people perform in categorization tasks. Thirdly, Labov's study suggests that the boundaries of such categories may be ill-defined and context-dependent.

Evidence like this led Rosch to conclude that people do not mentally represent categories in terms of defining features. Indeed, she proposed initially that lists of attributes play *no* part in these mental representations. Instead, she suggested that the conceptual representation of a given category is lodged in a **prototype**. Though it is difficult to specify exactly what this means, it is usually defined as a kind of composite which combines, in the form of a single 'mental blob', the characteristics of the most typical members of the category.

Rosch explicitly avoided any proposal about the *processes* by which instances are assigned to particular categories. The suggestion most frequently associated with the approach is that we estimate the overall similarity of a given item (say an odd, four-legged object) to the prototypes of different categories (say table, chair, etc.) and assign it to the category whose prototype it resembles most. This process of categorization is based on overall similarity, rather than any comparison of the individual features of object and prototype.

According to the prototype approach, people rate category members as good or poor exemplars (see Techniques Box B) because they mentally represent categories in terms of an abstraction based on typical members. A 'good' exemplar will be one which has a high degree of resemblance to the prototype; a 'poor' exemplar will be one with a low resemblance to the prototype. The reason why typicality affects the speed of tasks such as categorization of concept words (see Techniques Box C) is that a test item such as 'chair' which closely resembles the prototype for the target category 'furniture' will be more readily categorized than an item such as 'clock' which does not resemble the prototype very much.

The finding that categories have fuzzy boundaries (Section 3.3) is also in keeping with the prototype approach. The approach implies that people have a representation of what a typical cup is like (i.e. a prototype), rather than a definition as to what is a cup and what is a bowl. The effect of providing a context is presumably to *suggest* a possible categorization (cup, bowl or vase) for somewhat atypical objects. Provided the presented object bears some general resemblance to the prototype for this category, it can be included in the category.

The real problem with the prototype approach is the difficulty of specifying exactly what a prototype is. Assuming that it is a kind of 'composite' of the most typical members of a category, the prototype for a category such as 'fruit' should be a 'mental object' somewhere between an orange, an apple, a banana and other typical fruit. But if we try to imagine what such an item might be like, we come up with a rather weird object, which seems extremely atypical of the category. These difficulties led psychologists to abandon the original notion of a prototype as a single composite representation.

The next section will consider some attempts to accommodate evidence against the defining feature approach in models which try to specify the nature of conceptual representation more clearly than the original prototype approach.

Summary of Section 3

Evidence against the defining feature view of concept representation includes the following:

- Everyday categories such as 'chair' do not lend themselves to specification in terms of defining properties.
- Subjects can rate members of a category such as fruit or furniture according to how well they exemplify the category. One explanation is that the mental representations of these categories are internally structured according to the typicality of their members.
- Subjects can categorize typical category members more quickly than atypical category members. This suggests that typicality is fundamental to the way these categories are represented and hence that all category members do not have equal status.
- Context affects how subjects categorize pictures of everyday household objects. This suggests that the boundaries of such categories are fuzzy or ill-defined rather than clear-cut and well-defined.
- Rosch's prototype approach suggests that the conceptual representation of a given category is lodged in a prototype. This was initially assumed to be a composite, combining in a single mental entity the characteristics of the most typical category members.

4   Typical feature and exemplar models

In this section we shall look at some different attempts to reformulate the idea of a prototype. These are:

1 *The typical feature model*
   This model assumes that properties or features play a role in specifying categories. This role is not as a definition which applies equally to all category members, but as a list of typical features or properties which together represent what is most typical and distinctive of the category.

2 *The exemplar model*
   This model assumes that for each category there are a number of separate representations corresponding to specific exemplars that a person has encountered.

3 *Mixed approaches*
   These assume that categories are represented by a combination of typical feature and exemplar information.

4.1   The typical feature model

Many researchers have proposed typical feature models, and here we shall consider a representative version proposed by Rosch and Mervis (1975).

The core assumption of the **typical feature model** is that the mental representation of a concept consists of a list of properties or features, each with a 'weighting' termed a **cue validity** which indicates how characteristically the feature is associated with that concept. For instance, a feature such as 'sweet' is typically associated with the conceptual category 'fruit', and only rarely associated with the contrast category 'vegetable'. This feature is said to have a high cue validity for the concept fruit because it would be helpful in deciding whether an item was a fruit or vegetable. A feature such as 'crunchy', which is associated about equally with both fruit and vegetables, has a lower cue validity for fruit than 'sweet' because it would not be much use in deciding whether an item was a fruit or vegetable.

According to this model, typical members of the category are those which possess most of the features that have high cue validity for the category. For instance, 'orange' is a highly typical fruit because it possesses features such as 'juicy', 'sweet', 'pips', etc., each of which has a high weighting or high cue validity for fruit. 'Coconut' is a less typical fruit because it possesses fewer of these features with high cue validity.

SAQ 7
(a) The following are all properties or features which may be associated with the concept 'bird'. What do you think is the relative cue validity of the three features for the concept (i.e. which feature would be most useful and which least useful in deciding if a 'thing' was a bird)?

    Brown colour
    Feathers
    Flies

(b) Each of the following birds possesses two of the three properties listed under (a). Which bird has the pair of properties with the higher cue validity, and should therefore be more typical of the concept?

    Parrot
    Emu

An important implication of Rosch and Mervis's model is that typical category members will possess more features in common than atypical members, producing what they called a **family resemblance** structure within the category. In a family, some members share some features in common (e.g. brown eyes), others share others (e.g. blond hair). The closest members share more features in common, though no two members of the family (except identical twins) have an identical set of features. In the same way, typical category members are those with a high degree of family resemblance (i.e. many features in common with other members of the same category; few with members of contrast categories). Atypical members are those with a low degree of family resemblance (few features in common with other category members; many with members of contrast categories).

The specific evidence which led Rosch and Mervis to adopt this model is described in Techniques Box E. Subjects were asked to characterize superordinate categories such as 'fruit' by listing properties for each of the members ('apple', 'orange', etc.). This is similar to the listing of properties you carried out in Activities 1 and 2, except that in those Activities you were asked to focus on the properties of single members ('triangle', 'chair') of superordinate categories ('geometric figure', 'furniture').

TECHNIQUES BOX E

Properties of Everyday Category Members
(Rosch and Mervis, 1975)

Rationale
To investigate what role, if any, properties or features play in subjects' representations of everyday categories. Rosch and Mervis predicted that:

1 Subjects will use properties or features to characterize different category members, not listing exactly the same properties for all category members.

2 Subjects will tend to list the same or similar sets of properties for the most typical category members.

3 The properties listed for atypical category members will tend not to be those listed as shared by typical category members; in some cases these properties will overlap with those listed for contrast categories.

Method
Subjects were given randomly ordered lists of concepts belonging to superordinate categories such as fruit, vegetables, furniture. The concepts included ranged from highly typical items such as 'orange' to atypical items such as 'coconut', as rated in Rosch's earlier studies (see Techniques Box B). For each concept, subjects were asked to list the properties or features (such as 'juicy', 'sweet') they associated with it.

Results

On the whole, there was agreement amongst subjects on which properties they listed for particular category members. Thus, most subjects listed properties such as 'sweet', 'juicy', 'pips', 'round', for a highly typical fruit such as an orange. Subjects tended to list many, though not all, of the same properties for other typical category members; for instance, they listed 'sweet', 'juicy', and 'pips' for the concept 'grape'. Thus, typical category members tended to share some, if not all, of the same properties. For atypical category members, subjects listed few of these shared properties (e.g. only 'round' and 'sweet' for coconut), as well as some of the properties they listed for contrast categories (e.g. subjects listed 'hard' and 'fibrous' for coconut and also for vegetables such as carrot and celery).

Rosch and Mervis interpreted these results as being consistent with the general prototype approach, in showing that members of a category such as 'fruit' occupy differing rather than equivalent status, depending on how typical they are of the category. However, the fact that subjects in this experiment were *able* to list properties of category members was interpreted as supporting the typical feature model rather than the original prototype approach. The implication seemed to be that people's mental representation of a category such as 'fruit' consists, not of a single composite combining the characteristics of the most typical exemplars, but of a list of the individual features or properties which are common to the most typical members. The features on this list are those with high cue validity for the category (i.e. those which are typical and distinctive for the concept and therefore useful in deciding whether an item is a member or not).

4.2 *Evaluating the typical feature model*

The typical feature model was proposed as a refinement to Rosch's prototype approach. The most specific evidence for the model was presented in Techniques Box E, but we also need to assess the model's compatibility with the three main sets of results presented in Section 3, which support the fuzzy concept approach.

Typicality ratings (Techniques Box B)

The typical feature model is compatible with the finding that subjects rate category members as varying in typicality: they should be rated as typical if they possess features with high cue validity for the category; they should be rated atypical if they possess features with low cue validity for the category.

Effects of typicality on speed of categorizing
concept words (Techniques Box C)
The typical feature model can explain this finding by making the following general assumption about how an object possessing relevant features for a category such as 'chair' is actually categorized. The features of the object are compared with the stored feature list that represents 'chair' as well as with feature lists for contrast categories. For each feature of the object which matches a feature in the stored representation for 'chair', the appropriate cue validity is computed from the stored representation. The cue validities of all matched features are added together and if the sum of cue validities exceeds some threshold value for categorization as a chair, the instance is classified as an instance of this concept. Since typical items possess more of the features with high cue validity than do atypical items, accumulation of a total which exceeds the threshold will occur more quickly.

Effects of context on categorization (Techniques Box D)
Labov's finding that context can affect category boundaries is slightly more taxing for the model. A possible explanation is that the cue validities attached to particular features can actually be adjusted depending on context. For instance, if the context encourages a person to think that an object to be categorized is a receptacle for drinking coffee, he or she may attach less importance to whether it has a handle or not than in a 'neutral' condition where context does not create a bias in one direction or another. If the effect of the context is strong enough, the object may be classified as a 'cup' even if it does not have a handle. Effectively, the cue validity of a handle as a feature which is important in identifying cups could thus be lowered.

The model is therefore consistent with the main experimental findings, but it poses some important theoretical problems. For one thing, it implies that people's knowledge of particular categories is confined to *lists* of their features. But in practice people also know a lot about the *relationship* between specific features. For instance, our knowledge of chairs includes information about how characteristic features are related to each other. Having a flat surface is a typical feature of tables as well as chairs, but having a flat surface joined at an angle to a straight backrest is only typical of chairs. It could be argued that by combining these individual features together into larger 'units', one is identifying *higher order features* which help to characterize a concept. These higher order features in which the structural arrangement of parts are specified are known as **structural descriptions**. They prove to be particularly important in the perceptual categorization of objects (see Part II, Section 5.2 of this book).

At the same time, the model fails to specify *components* of features which may help to characterize a concept; that is, it implies that concepts are mentally represented by units of the size which Rosch's subjects listed in her experiments. In practice, people may differentiate these 'features' into smaller units which play a significant role in representation. For instance, wings are a feature of both birds and bats. But the components of bird wings and bat wings are quite different: a bat wing consists of a web of skin stretched over a bony frame; a bird wing has feathers attached to bones similar in structure to those in the human arm and wrist. Thus, a common 'feature' of bats and birds can be broken down into smaller features which differentiate between the two categories. Basic units or elements which differentiate categories are known as **primitives**. Again, in the perceptual categorization of objects, it is very important that primitives are specified at the right level (see Part II, Section 5.1).

4.3   The exemplar model

Both Rosch's original prototype approach and the typical feature model assume that categories are represented by some sort of generalized abstraction based on the characteristics of the most typical members. In the case of the prototype approach, this was a single composite based on typical members, whereas, in the typical feature model, it consisted of a list of the most typical features. In contrast, the **exemplar model** (e.g. Smith and Medin, 1981; Hintzman, 1988; Barsalou, 1992) assumes that the category representation consists of individual representations of some of the exemplars a person has encountered, stored in memory. Thus, for instance, my representation for the category 'chair' might consist of the following exemplars:

A chair from my dining room
The chair I work on in the library
The chair at my dressing table
Etc.

The difference between the two models is depicted in schematic form in Figure 1.7 overleaf, which shows how the concept 'chair' might be represented within the typical feature approach and the exemplar approach.

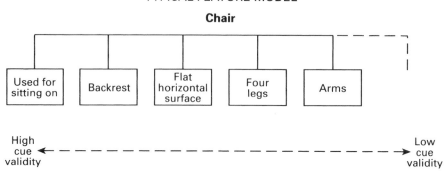

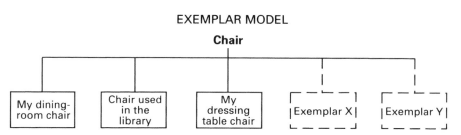

Figure 1.7 Schematic illustration of representations for 'chair' within typical feature and exemplar models

4.4 Evaluating the exemplar model

One advantage of the exemplar approach emerges from Figure 1.7: it provides a way of storing adequate information about categories whose exemplars vary a lot from one another. Take the superordinate category 'furniture'. Even typical exemplars such as chair, table and desk vary in the features which describe them, and atypical members such as 'clock' may share very little in common with these typical members. It may be implausible to suggest that a single feature list, albeit weighted towards the more typical category members, could represent the category as a whole. The exemplar model solves this problem by allowing multiple representations, each based on a *different* category member.

This, however, poses a problem: how, if at all, to impose constraints on how many different exemplars of a category are stored. Storing multiple exemplars requires a large amount of memory capacity and appears to violate the general requirement of *cognitive economy* —

that categories should be represented in a manner which stores adequate information with minimum effort (see Section 1.1).

One version of the exemplar model (e.g. Hintzman, 1988) simply overrides this requirement and assumes that a person stores exemplars of every instance previously encountered. Hintzman argues that, since the capacity of long-term memory is supposedly unlimited, advantages of preserving detailed information in this way may outweigh the disadvantages in terms of economy of representation. However, this appears to pose a further problem: no two people's representations of a concept need be the same, because the representations will be idiosyncratic to the extent that each of these individuals has encountered different exemplars in his or her lifetime. In practice, however, the different concept representations held by different individuals do share much in common.

To meet these objections to this 'unlimited' exemplar model, another class of exemplar model assumes that it *is* necessary to constrain which exemplars are stored. One such model described by Smith and Medin (1981) assumes that the representation is restricted to the most typical exemplars of the concept (i.e. those which meet a particular criterion for numbers of properties shared with other exemplars). Within this model, the stored exemplars of, say, 'furniture' would be restricted to items such as chair, table and desk, which are typical exemplars of the concept.

By way of further evaluation, we can compare this 'limited' exemplar model with the main empirical phenomena of the fuzzy concept approach.

Typicality ratings (Techniques Box B)
Assuming that the representation of the concept consists of the most typical exemplars, an instance which matches or is very similar to one of these exemplars will be rated as typical, whereas an instance which shares little in common with any of these exemplars will be rated atypical.

Effects of typicality on speed of categorizing
concept words (Techniques Box C)
This result can be explained by making the following assumption about how newly encountered items are categorized: a description of such an item is compared simultaneously to exemplars of those categories stored in memory. The item is assigned to the category whose exemplars it resembles most. As typical items have a higher degree of resemblance to the stored exemplars of their category, the accumulation of some criterion level of resemblance will be achieved faster than where the item to be categorized is atypical.

Effects of context on categorization (Techniques Box D)

SAQ 8
See if you can derive an explanation for fuzzy boundaries and context effects (see Techniques Box D) from the exemplar model.

Both unlimited and limited exemplar models share the problem that they are unspecific about the nature of the exemplar representations: in what way are the individual exemplars selected for the representation actually stored inside a person's head? Two possibilities are that the exemplars are represented as mental images or that they are represented as feature lists. Researchers appear to favour the second possibility, but in so doing blur the distinction between the exemplar model and the alternative typical feature model.

4.5   Comparing models

We have now considered three different approaches — the prototype approach, the typical feature model, and the exemplar model — all of which assume that concepts are represented not as sets of defining characteristics but in some more 'fuzzy' way. At this stage, it may be useful to summarize the key points of these approaches (see Table 1.4).

As Table 1.4 shows, the three approaches can be distinguished in terms of their assumptions about the nature of representation and the mode of categorization, and each approach has some different theoretical problems. What is striking, however, is that the approaches do not differ very significantly in their compatibility with the main classes of empirical data. This seems highly unsatisfactory, since one should be able to choose between models on the basis of how well they account for empirical evidence. Researchers have responded to this 'impasse' in one of two ways. The first, which we shall consider in the remainder of this section, is to suggest that we do not need to choose between models because the forms of mental representation they postulate will operate *jointly*; that is, in representing a category such as 'chair', a person will adopt a combination of generalized summary information (a prototype or a feature list) *and* specific exemplar information. This suggestion retains the general assumption that concepts are represented in some 'fuzzy' form.

Other recent researchers, whose work we will consider in the final sections of this chapter, suggest that a more radical rethink of the whole field is required.

Table 1.4   Fuzzy concept approaches

Approach	Nature of representation	How an instance is categorized	Which empirical findings are explained	Theoretical problems
Original prototype	Composite abstraction based on most typical members	By measuring overall similarity of instance to category prototypes	Typicality ratings; typicality effects (e.g. speed of categorization); context effects	Nature of prototype not clear
Typical feature model	List of features abstracted from typical instances and weighted according to strength of association	By comparing features of instance with feature lists for categories and computing the sum of cue validities for the instance.	Typicality ratings; typicality effects (e.g. speed of categorization); ?context effects	Feature lists do not represent relations between features or components of features.
Exemplar model	Individual representations of exemplars the person has encountered	By comparing the instance to the multiple exemplar representations for different categories and assigning to the category whose exemplars it most closely resembles	The 'limited' exemplar model explains: typicality ratings; typicality effects (e.g. speed of categorization); context effects	How are exemplars actually stored?

4.6   'Mixed' approaches

There is both anecdotal and experimental evidence to suggest that people employ a mixture of representations for categories. Anecdotal support (Barsalou, 1992) is provided by the fact that, when we ask people what they know about a category such as 'dog', it is quite clear that they have general summary-type information (dogs are animals with four legs; they bark) as well as knowledge of specific exemplars (my dog 'Towser'; the neighbour's large Alsatian, etc.). Adults employ both types of information when teaching children about new concepts. They may tell children about typical features (birds fly and say 'tweet tweet'), but they also point out exemplars ('There is a bird').

Experimental evidence comes from studies in which subjects are asked to familiarize themselves with specific categories by categorizing a set of 'training' exemplars. Their performance in categorizing further exemplars is then investigated. By manipulating the characteristics of these new exemplars, one can evaluate the relative importance of general summary information (a prototype or a feature list) and specific exemplar information in subjects' categorization performance (see Techniques Box F). Notice that this experiment does not distinguish between prototype and typical feature lists, treating them both as generalized summary representations, in contrast to exemplar representations which are assumed to consist of unsummarized information about specific exemplars.

TECHNIQUES BOX F

The Use of Generalized Summary Versus Exemplar Information in Categorizing Objects (Jacoby and Brooks, 1984)

Rationale
To investigate the contribution of prototype or typical feature list vs. exemplar information to subjects' ability to categorize pictorially presented instances of everyday categories.

Method

1 Training phase:
Subjects were shown 12 slides depicting objects, as follows:

9 slides depicted instances of each of the three categories 'cup', 'bottle', 'glass'.

The remaining 3 slides depicted glass objects which were non-members of these categories.

The 12 slides were presented in random order. Each slide presentation was preceded by the question 'Is it a cup (bottle/glass)?'. Subjects answered 'yes' or 'no' as quickly as possible on seeing the slide.

2 Test phase:
Subjects performed the same task with 39 further slides, as follows:

12 Training Phase (TP) slides — training phase slides repeated.

12 New Similar (NS) slides — new items clearly similar to those in the training phase.

12 New Different (ND) slides — new items clearly different from those in the training phase.

3 New Typical (NT) slides — one highly typical (previously unseen) item for each of the categories, cup, bottle, and glass.

For example:

TP item	NS item	ND item	NT item
Child's yellow cup with a lion painted on it.	Child's blue cup, same shape, with dog painted on it, lying sideways.	Adult's fluted coffee cup, abstract design.	Adult's teacup, typical shape, with Willow Pattern design.

Results (times to categorize items in milliseconds):

Training phase	Test phase			
(TP)	(TP)	(NS)	(ND)	(NT)
268	214	225	278	237

Not surprisingly, in the test phase subjects categorized the (repeated) TP items fastest. More interesting is the fact that NS and NT items were categorized faster than ND items, although none of these items had previously been seen by subjects. NS and NT items were also categorized faster than the TP items in the training phase.

Conclusion
During the training phase, subjects were extracting both general summary information (prototype or feature list) and information about individual exemplars. Subjects used the former information to form a generalized summary representation of what is typical about the category, and this facilitated their identification of new but highly typical (NT) instances. Subjects used the latter information to form a representation consisting of multiple individual exemplars, and this facilitated their subsequent identification of new items (NS) which were similar to previously seen instances.

In conclusion, this evidence suggests that subjects store a mixture of representations for everyday concepts such as 'cup' or 'glass'. They acquire both a prototype or feature list summarizing what is most typical about the category, and information about specific exemplars. Both types of information are called on in categorizing new instances. While acknowledging that more than one type of representation is employed, this approach remains within the broad framework that assumes that concept representations are in general 'fuzzy' rather than definitional. The next section will look at some more recent work which reconsiders this general picture.

Summary of Section 4

- The typical feature model assumes that conceptual categories are each represented by a list of the features most typically associated with a category. Each feature is listed with a weighting or cue validity which indicates how characteristically the feature is associated with the category.

- Specific evidence for this model comes from studies in which subjects list properties of the members of everyday categories. They list many shared features for typical members and few for atypical members. The features listed for atypical members overlap with those listed for members of contrast categories.

- The model is compatible with experimental results, but fails to allow for relationships among features, known as structural descriptions, and components of features, known as primitives.

- The exemplar model assumes that conceptual categories are each represented by some or all of the exemplars a person has encountered.

- The 'unlimited' exemplar model appears to violate the principle of cognitive economy and fails to explain how different people come to have similar conceptual representations.

- The 'limited' exemplar model assumes that concept representations are confined to the most typical exemplars. This model is compatible with the main experimental results, but raises the question of how exemplars are actually stored.

- Both anecdotal and experimental evidence suggests that people acquire a combination of general summary information in the form of a prototype or typical feature list, and specific exemplar information, in order to represent concepts and to categorize new instances.

5   Concept representations for different purposes

In Section 2 of this part we considered a class of entities — geometric figures — which seem well-defined in themselves. The fact that there are widely agreed rules for describing concepts such as 'triangle', 'quadrilateral', etc. suggested that the mental representations for such figures may take a definitional form.

Rosch set out to demonstrate that this approach is inadequate as a general account of how people represent concepts. However, her studies employed conceptual categories which do not seem well-defined in themselves. It does not necessarily follow that *all* concept representations must be ill-defined or fuzzy. This section will pursue the theme that well-defined and fuzzy representations for concepts are not mutually exclusive alternatives. Two important factors determining the type of representation employed in a particular context are: the purposes for which the representation is used, and the individual knowledge of the 'user'.

5.1   The basic level

Rosch (Rosch et al., 1976) suggested that there is one level within conceptual hierarchies at which category members possess relatively many properties in common with each other, as well as relatively few in common with contrast categories. This level is known as the **basic level**. This proposal modifies rather than contradicts Rosch's claim that categories are ill-defined with fuzzy boundaries: at one level — the basic level — categories are *less* fuzzy and ill-defined than at other levels. This is because they serve the special purpose of summarizing information about particular domains in the most economical way for cognitive activities, including memory, perception and communication.

The original evidence for the basic level came from studies by the anthropologist Berlin (1972) of how plants are classified by cultural groups such as the Tzeltal Indians of Mexico. Berlin noted that the category names which are most used in such cultures tend to be confined to categories at a particular level in the scientific classification of plants. For instance, in the case of trees, the cultures studied by Berlin tended to have terms for 'genera' such as beech or birch rather than for general superordinate groupings or individual species such as silver birch or copper beech. According to Berlin, this is because categories such as 'birch' and 'beech' are naturally distinctive and coherent groupings — the species they include tend to have common patterns of features such as leaf shape, bark colour, and so on.

Rosch and her colleagues argued that the principle of a basic level would be a general property of human categorization, applying not only to the botanical categories studied by Berlin (e.g. tree) but also to objects constructed by people (artefacts such as musical instruments, tools, furniture and clothing), types of food (e.g. fruit and vegetables), and zoological categories (e.g. fish, bird).

Figure 1.8 overleaf illustrates two of the three-level hierarchies investigated by Rosch. One is a biological taxonomy of birds, though missing many of the levels which ornithologists use in classifying birds. The other is a hierarchy of everyday objects, namely furniture.

SAQ 9
According to Berlin's findings, which level should be basic for the bird hierarchy shown in Figure 1.8? Which level would you intuitively predict to be basic for the furniture hierarchy?

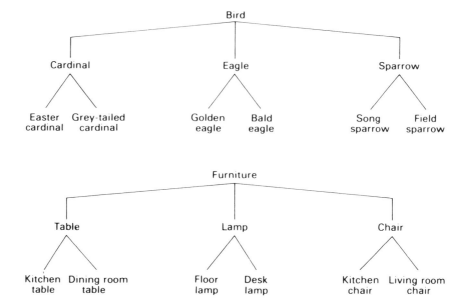

Figure 1.8 Rosch's hierarchies for birds and for furniture (note: birds shown are native to North America rather than Great Britain)   (based on Rosch et al., 1976, Table 1)

Rosch's investigations of the basic level are discussed in Techniques Box G.

TECHNIQUES BOX G

Listings of Properties for Basic Level Categories
(Rosch et al., 1976)

Rationale

To investigate the properties which people list for categories at three different levels in conceptual hierarchies. There is predicted to be one level at which subjects list many properties which are both characteristic (common to most category members) and distinctive (not shared by members of other categories). This level is predicted to be the intermediate level.

Method

As in Techniques Box E, subjects were presented with lists of category items and asked to list the properties they associate with each. The hierarchies investigated included artefacts (musical instruments, tools, furniture, clothing), types of food (fruit, vegetables) and biological categories (tree, fish and bird). For a given hierarchy, the

---

presented items included the superordinate (e.g. 'bird'), intermediate members ('sparrow', 'robin', etc.), and subordinates ('song sparrow', 'field sparrow', etc.).

Results
Table 1.5 shows a sample of results for the 'furniture' and 'bird' hierarchies. As predicted, at the intermediate level in the 'furniture' hierarchy (i.e. for the category 'chair'), subjects listed a relatively large number of properties, which they also listed for many of the subordinate categories

Table 1.5

Level	Everyday		Biological	
	Category	properties listed	Category	properties listed
Superordinate	Furniture	None	Bird	Feathers Head Wings Claws Beak Lays Legs eggs Feet Nests Eyes Flies Tail Chirps Eats flies and worms
Intermediate (predicted basic level)	Chair	Legs Seat Back Arms Comfortable Four legs Wood For sitting on	Sparrow	As for 'Bird' Small Brown
Subordinate	Living room chair	As for 'Chair' plus: Large Soft Cushion	Song sparrow	As for 'Sparrow'
	Kitchen chair	As for 'Chair'	Field sparrow	As for 'Sparrow'

(shown for 'living room chair', 'kitchen chair'). Thus, whereas subjects listed no attributes for 'furniture', they listed eight attributes for 'chair' and also listed these for 'living room chair' and 'kitchen chair'. Only three additional attributes are listed for 'living room chair', and none for 'kitchen chair'. A similar pattern of results occurred for the other non-biological categories, though 'furniture' was the only superordinate for which subjects listed no attributes at all.

For the 'bird' hierarchy, it was the superordinate category rather than the intermediate category for which subjects listed numerous characteristic and distinctive properties. This pattern of results was common to the three biological hierarchies.

Conclusion
Rosch concluded that a basic level existed for both the biological and non-biological hierarchies. But her prediction that the intermediate level would be basic was only confirmed for the non-biological hierarchies. It is clear that, for the biological hierarchies, Rosch's subjects, unlike Berlin's, treated the superordinate level categories as basic.

SAQ 10
Can you suggest a reason why the basic level was different for Rosch's and Berlin's subjects?

Rosch et al.'s studies of the basic level also showed that the basic level is the highest one in a hierarchy at which category members are judged to look alike. Thus, members of the category 'chair' are judged to look alike, whereas members of the category 'furniture' are not. This may indicate that the basic level is the highest level at which people can form a generalized image of the category. Similarly, Rosch et al. found that the basic level is the most inclusive level at which people associate similar movements with category members. For instance, the same sitting movement is associated with many different kinds of chairs. There is no common movement associated with different types of furniture.

These findings confirm the prediction that one level within conceptual hierarchies will serve as the basic level: the relatively good definition at this level makes it the most informative and economical for cognitive activities such as memory, perception, and communication. If we use a basic level concept such as 'apple' for cognition and communication, this conveys much more information than if we use 'fruit'. If we use the term 'Cox's apple', this may give more information than is really required.

Throughout our earlier discussion, the category 'chair' has been given as an example of an everyday category which is difficult to define and which shows some features in common with contrast categories such as seat, stool, etc. None the less, as a basic level category, 'chair' has a number of properties which are *highly* characteristic and distinctive. Activity 2 in Section 3.1 would have been even more difficult if the category to be described had been 'furniture', which is a very diffuse, ill-defined category, or 'dining chair', which shares so much in common with 'kitchen chair', etc.

5.2   *Expert and everyday representations*

Rosch's studies of the basic level concern the relatively well-defined characteristics of one hierarchical level compared with others. Other researchers have focused on the fact that a single concept can lend itself to both a fuzzy representation and a representation in terms of defining features. These alternative representations may be held by different people, or by the same person for use on different occasions. These proposals bring in the important role of **expert knowledge** in producing variations in how a given domain is represented.

A chemist may categorize substances such as lead, copper, gold, etc. in terms of defining features such as the numbers of electrons, protons and neutrons in their atoms, whereas people with no scientific expertise may have much less precise concepts of these substances. Conversely, it is sometimes the layperson who divides the world into clear-cut categories, while the expert with greater knowledge may treat category distinctions as fuzzy. For instance, we divide up the world into living things and non-living things, whereas scientists are aware that particles such as viruses do not fall clearly into either category. A similar point applies to concept pairs such as 'life' and 'death', 'male' and 'female'. We behave as if there were clear-cut boundaries between these categories, yet the definitions of these boundaries are the subject of much debate in medical and legal circles.

Confirmation of this effect of expert knowledge on categorization comes from a study by Murphy and Wright (1984). They compared concepts of various psychiatric disorders held by experts and novices. They reported that the experts' concepts were actually less distinctive and clear-cut, and concluded that greater knowledge may have led the experts to focus on the *shared* rather than the distinctive features of the disorders.

Not only may different people differ in their expertise, but the same person may hold a **dual representation** of the same concept — a 'fuzzy' one for everyday purposes, and a precise definition which can be called for when precision is required. An elegant illustration of this proposal is provided by Armstrong et al. (1983). Take the concept 'grandmother'. Instances of this concept tend typically to share perceptual and functional properties, such as grey hair, wrinkles and a twinkle in the eye. Not all members of the class will have these properties, and some may have more of them than others. This is precisely what Rosch's studies of property listings imply. However, while Rosch's work might suggest that a person's only representation for the concept 'grandmother' would be a list of these typical properties, Armstrong et al. argued that this list may be merely a superficial representation used to make quick judgements of which individuals are likely to belong to the category 'grandmother'. People may also possess a more precise representation of the category, sometimes known as a **conceptual core**. For 'grandmother', this conceptual core will be 'mother of a parent': this is a definition which applies equally to all category members.

There may even be several different degrees of precision in representing concepts. For instance, the concept 'gold' may be represented in the following three ways:

1 Yellow glittery stuff.
2 Precious yellow non-rusting malleable ductile metal.
3 Atomic number 79.

The first representation serves for everyday purposes, in that it serves to distinguish gold from non-gold on a rough-and-ready basis. The second representation has the degree of precision which a layperson might use when precision is called for — although it may not distinguish gold from non-gold on absolutely all occasions. The third representation is a 'factual scientific description' — sometimes termed a **real essence**. The third representation comes closest to the traditional notion of a necessary and sufficient property which applies to all gold and only to gold, though according to contemporary scientific thought even these most clear-cut 'definitions' are potentially fallible.

It does not necessarily follow that *all* concepts are represented by *all* people in two, let alone three, ways. For instance, as Armstrong et al. point out, 'few other than vintners and certain biologists may have much in the way of a serious description of "grape" mentally represented' (i.e. in such cases, the fuzzy representation may serve as the *only* representation of the concept). By the same token, we might intuitively predict that *obviously* well-defined concepts such as geometric figures are mentally represented only in definitional form. Yet, as we shall see next, Armstrong et al. (1983) found evidence which suggested that these well-defined concepts can also lend themselves to fuzzy representations.

5.3   Fuzzy representations for well-defined concepts?

In Section 3.1, it was noted that the everyday categories studied by Rosch do not seem well-defined in themselves. The fact that they cannot be readily specified externally by defining properties is mirrored, according to Rosch, by fuzzy mental representations centred on the characteristics of typical members. Typicality effects are seen as a direct reflection of this form of representation.

What is more surprising is that typicality effects appear to occur for obviously well-defined domains. The experiments in which Armstrong et al. (1983) made this finding are described in Techniques Box H.

TECHNIQUES BOX H

Typicality Effects with Well-defined Concepts
(Armstrong et al., 1983)

Rationale
To investigate whether typicality effects occur for 'well-defined' categories as well as 'everyday' categories.

Method
Experiment 1
Subjects were run on a replication of Rosch's typicality rating experiments (cf. Techniques Box B). Categories employed were of two types:

Everyday	Sport	Vehicle	Fruit	Vegetable
Well-defined	Odd number	Even number	Female	Geometric figure

Experiment 2
Using the same materials, subjects were run on a replication of a sentence verification task (cf. Techniques Box A). Subjects had to verify sentences such as 'An orange is a fruit', in which instances were either good or poor exemplars of their categories as rated in Experiment 1.

Experiment 3
A new set of subjects were asked outright whether membership of the categories (fruit, odd number, etc.) is a matter of degree. They were then re-run on Experiment 1.

Results
Experiment 1
Subjects produced typicality ratings for items from both everyday and well-defined categories. It apparently made sense to judge certain odd numbers or geometric figures as good examples of their category (e.g. '3' was rated as a better example of an odd number than '23')

Experiment 2
Typicality effects occurred for both everyday and well-defined categories (i.e. subjects verified statements about odd numbers faster if the items in the statements had been judged typical in Experiment 1).

Experiment 3
When a new set of subjects was asked outright if membership of well-defined categories is a matter of degree, they denied it. Yet they still produced typicality ratings when tested in Experiment 1.

Armstrong et al.'s interpretation of these findings is that people have 'fuzzy' representations constructed from the properties of typical members, even for categories such as odd numbers or geometric figures which seem obviously well-defined. For instance, since subjects judged 'square' to be a good example of a geometric figure, whereas 'ellipse' was judged to be a poor example, this implies that they possess a representation for the category 'geometric figure' which is much more like a square than an ellipse. Yet these same subjects were clearly aware that membership of the category 'geometric figure' is not, logically, a matter of degree — a figure either is or is not a member of this category. Apparently, people therefore possess dual representations, even for these obviously well-defined categories.

One problem with this interpretation is that it does not seem cognitively economical to have dual representations, one of which is, logically speaking, incorrect. If we are well aware that membership of the category 'odd numbers' is not, in reality, a matter of degree, what is the advantage of thinking of the category in this way? The suggested answer is that, as for 'grandmother', fuzzy representations for well-defined concepts provide a basis for rapid everyday judgements. If you are asked to explain what a geometric figure is, for many purposes it may be quite sufficient to think of the properties which typical exemplars such as squares and triangles have. It would probably take longer to work out a formal definition which applies to all geometric figures, and it might be less readily understood by the layperson. On the other hand, if you were having a conversation with a philosopher or mathematician, it would certainly be advisable to have your core definition of a geometric figure to the fore! In conclusion, though a dual representation may be less economical in terms of memory storage, for other cognitive purposes it may be more economical to have alternative representations which are specifically tailored for different types of thinking and which can be readily shared by lay people or experts respectively.

Findings like those of Armstrong et al. undermine the original clarity of the fuzzy concept approach, since they question Rosch's assumption that the nature of a concept representation can be inferred from people's performance in typicality experiments. This has led researchers such as Lakoff (1987) to argue that, although they are real, typicality effects are 'superficial' — that is, they do not tell us anything straightforward about how people represent concepts. The next and final section explores further the complex relationship between typicality effects and concept representation.

Summary of Section 5

- Within conceptual hierarchies there is one level at which the categories are both more informative and more economical than at other levels. This level serves a special purpose as the basic level for cognitive activities such as perception, memory, and communication.
- Basic level categories represent the highest level in hierarchies at which categories have many properties in common and few in common with contrast categories. They are thus relatively well-defined.
- According to the dual representation approach, many concepts lend themselves to two or more representations — a 'fuzzy' representation which serves as a basis for quick everyday judgements, and a conceptual core which is used if precise or expert definition is called for.
- Even obviously well-defined concepts such as geometric figures are subject to typicality effects, suggesting the existence of dual representations.
- Findings such as these suggest (a) that the purposes for which representations are used and differences in the knowledge held by individuals must be taken into account in making predictions about how concepts are represented, and (b) that the relationship between typicality and concept representation is not straightforward.

6   Diversity and flexibility in conceptual representation

The major approaches reviewed earlier in this chapter — the defining feature approach and the fuzzy concept approach — made two implicit assumptions. The first was that the general character of conceptual representation (definitional according to one view, fuzzy according to the other) will be the same for many different types of concept, the different individuals who possess the representations, and the different purposes for which they are used. The second was that concept representations exist in long-term memory as relatively stable, static structures.

Yet in Section 4 we saw that people employ a mixture of representations for everyday concepts, and in Section 5 we saw that the nature of concept representations varies according to their level within a hierarchy, the person who holds the representation (expert or non-expert), and the context in which the representation is used (formal thinking or everyday communication). These findings argue for diversity and flexibility in the way concepts are represented, and this argument has been extended in recent work by Barsalou (1991).

6.1   *Taxonomic and goal-directed categories*

Barsalou distinguishes two major types of conceptual category. The first, which he refers to as **taxonomic categories** are common categories of the kind discussed so far in this chapter (apple, fruit, bird, animal, triangle, geometric figure). These categories all share the property that they arise from experience; that is, acquisition of such categories, in childhood or adulthood, relies at least in part on experience of actual instances and their characteristics. The child acquires knowledge of a concept such as 'bird' by inspecting instances pointed out by a parent, and by what the parent says about these instances. From this experience, the child formulates a generalized representation of characteristic features as well as multiple representations of specific exemplars, as described in Section 4.6.

While most studies of conceptual representation are based on taxonomic categories, so-called **goal-directed categories** can also be seen as playing a major role in cognition. These are categories which a person might derive in order to achieve a specific plan or goal. Suppose, for instance, that a person is planning a trip to the highlands of Scotland. He/she might construct categories such as:

Things to pack for unpredictable weather.

Places of interest to visit.

Departure times that fit in with work.

Many such categories are ***ad hoc***; that is, they are temporary categories, derived impromptu by the individual in order to serve a particular goal. Moreover, experience with exemplars and their characteristics is not necessary in order to derive such categories. Instead, category acquisition occurs by a process of **conceptual combination** in which existing concepts are put together in a novel way in order to meet the particular goal the person has in mind.

Supposing that a person sets him/herself the goal of losing weight by going on a slimming diet. An *ad hoc* category 'Foods to eat on a slimming diet' would be created for this purpose. The person's knowledge of which foods fall into this category need not depend on previous direct experience of possible exemplars. Instead, the person combines information drawn from other taxonomic categories (e.g. 'food', 'diet') in order to identify the properties which exemplars should have (e.g. 'highly nutritious', 'low calorie', 'bulky') as well as exemplars which actually possess these attributes (e.g. 'brown bread', 'cabbage', etc.).

Barsalou (1983) has demonstrated that the representations which people possess for these *ad hoc*, goal-directed categories superficially mimic those associated with taxonomic categories. Thus, subjects are able to list properties for *ad hoc* category exemplars, as they did for

Rosch's studies of taxonomic categories (see Techniques Box E). Some of the category exemplars are assigned more shared properties than others, suggesting that people treat such categories as having internal structure. This is confirmed by the finding that subjects produce ordered typicality ratings for *ad hoc* category members, just as they do for taxonomic categories (Barsalou, 1983). However, Barsalou (1991) has also shown that the basis for this typicality structure differs from that in taxonomic categories. In taxonomic categories, exemplars are thought of as typical to the extent that they possess the most *representative* features of the category. Thus, vegetables such as pea or carrot are rated as typical because they possess many of the most characteristic features of the category ('crunchy', 'juicy', etc.). By contrast, exemplars of goal-directed categories are treated as typical to the extent that they approximate to the *ideal* for the category. Thus, for the category 'Foods to eat on a slimming diet', people tend to treat foods such as 'green pepper', 'grapefruit', etc. as highly typical. These exemplars approximate to the *ideal* of the category (i.e. they are nutritious and low in calories), although they do not necessarily have the most characteristic set of properties. The implication of these findings, as for the findings discussed in Section 5.3, is that the relationship between typicality and conceptual representation is complex: diverse types of category display typicality.

6.2   Stability in taxonomic and goal-directed categories

The most important difference between taxonomic and goal-directed categories is in the extent to which they are well established in memory.

First of all, to what extent are taxonomic categories stable? A study by Barsalou and Sewell (1984) showed that the internal structure of such categories is not entirely fixed. Subjects drawn from an American population were presented with members of everyday categories such as birds and asked to rate the typicality of members ('robin', 'eagle', 'parrot', etc.).

One group of subjects was asked to judge the typicality of the birds from the point of view of the average American citizen. Another group was asked to judge the typicality of the birds from the point of view of the average Chinese citizen. The results showed that the rated orders of typicality (from typical to least typical exemplars) varied significantly with the imagined point of view for the task. For instance, whereas 'robin' was treated as typical from the point of view of an American, and 'swan' as atypical, the order was reversed when subjects approached the task from the 'Chinese' point of view.

Barsalou and Sewell interpreted these results as showing that people are able to reorganize conceptual information in order to meet the particular purposes of the task. The results indicate flexibility in the way representations of everyday categories are employed, but do not necessarily imply that such categories are not well established in memory. The subjects in the task were American, and presumably treated the 'Chinese point of view' as a cue to temporarily reorganize their own relatively stable 'American' representation. It is interesting to note too that some of the American subjects' 'Chinese' typicality ratings reflected cultural stereotypes. Though the subjects tended to agree on what the stereotypes were (e.g. that Chinese people think of swans as typical birds), their ratings did not always match authentic typicality ratings obtained from Chinese subjects.

Ad hoc, goal-directed categories are by their very nature likely to be less well established in memory, and this was confirmed experimentally in a study in which subjects were presented with category exemplars for both taxonomic and *ad hoc* categories, and asked to suggest appropriate category labels (i.e. parent categories). This study is described in Techniques Box I.

TECHNIQUES BOX I

Generating Category Labels for Taxonomic and *Ad Hoc*
Categories (Barsalou, 1983)

Rationale
To investigate subjects' ability to generate appropriate category labels for *ad hoc* and taxonomic categories. Barsalou argued that taxonomic categories are relatively well established in memory, whereas *ad hoc* categories are poorly established. From this he predicted that:
1 For taxonomic categories, subjects will have no difficulty in generating appropriate category labels (i.e. parent categories).
2 For *ad hoc* categories, subjects will have difficulty generating appropriate labels, unless they are provided with contextual cues which indicate the goal or purpose of the categories.

Method
Subjects were supplied with lists of examples for the following three category types and asked to respond by supplying appropriate category labels:

Category type	Examples	Appropriate response (category label)
Taxonomic	apple, orange, banana, peach	Fruit
Ad hoc	get involved in local politics, get rich, have a garage sale, go to school	Ways to make friends
Random (control)	blue, erase, riddle, monkey	?

In order to tackle this task, half the subjects were provided with contextual cues to 'orient' them towards appropriate categories. Extracts from these cues are as follows:

Taxonomic: fruit:
Dan thoroughly enjoyed fruit. His favourite time of the year was summer because of the abundance of fresh fruit that was available.

Ad hoc: ways to make friends:
Martin had moved to the west coast . . . He had encountered trouble making friends . . . decided it was time to do something about it.

Random:
Horace was designing a computer system that would operate the traffic signal system in a major urban area . . .

The remaining subjects tackled the task without the assistance of such contextual cues.

Results
As predicted, subjects had no difficulty in generating appropriate labels for the taxonomic category items. The presence of a contextual cue had little effect on this generation, implying that these categories are well established in memory anyway. In contrast, subjects showed difficulty in generating appropriate labels for the *ad hoc* categories unless a contextual cue indicating the purpose of the category was supplied. For the random categories, subjects generated few labels, with or without a contextual cue.

Overall, these results support Barsalou's claim that, whereas taxonomic categories are relatively well established representations in memory, goal-directed categories are ill-established, being temporarily formulated to serve particular goals.

He concluded that the two types of category serve different but related functions in the representation of knowledge. People use taxonomic categories to build overall representations of the environment as they know it. For instance, a person's knowledge of animals is represented in memory as a set of hierarchically related categories reflecting to a greater or lesser extent the actual relations between animal species in the real world. People use goal-directed categories to link up these established representations with temporary categories containing **event frames** for achieving goals. Thus, the category 'horse' may be incorporated as part of the event frame 'going on a riding holiday'. Goal-directed categories enable people to *act* appropriately on their environment.

6.3   Conclusion

Barsalou's work is not only of interest in its own right, but crystallizes many of the points which cropped up in earlier sections. We started out with the apparently parsimonious claim that a single type of defining feature representation will be appropriate for different types of concept, used by different people in different contexts. Rosch's fuzzy concept approach was almost equally ambitious in claiming that most concepts lend themselves to a single type of fuzzy representation. It was not too surprising to find that both types of representation play a role in conceptual representation and that factors such as the type of concept, the individual who is using it, and the purposes for which it is used must all be taken into account. Barsalou's work indicates just how diverse concepts can be and what implications for conceptual representation arise from the different roles they play in cognition and communication. Along the way, we have seen that care is needed in the interpretation of all-pervasive typicality effects: the precise implications of these effects vary with the type of concepts for which they occur.

Summary of Section 6

• Barsalou has identified two different types of conceptual category. Taxonomic categories, for entities such as animals, furniture, or geometric figures, are acquired by direct experience with exemplars, and provide representations of the world as we know it. Goal-directed categories are formed, often *ad hoc*, to achieve particular goals. Their formation does not depend on direct experience of exemplars but on conceptual combination of information from other categories.

- Both types of category display typicality effects, though the under-lying basis differs for the two types. The most typical members of taxonomic categories are those with the most representative proper-ties. For goal-directed categories, the most typical members are those which correspond to the ideal for the category.

- Taxonomic categories are relatively well established in memory, though they may be deployed flexibly to suit different purposes. Goal-directed categories are not well established in memory. The two types of category serve different but related purposes in cognition.

- Barsalou's work highlights the importance of appreciating the di-verse nature of categories and their functions in establishing models of conceptual representation.

Further reading

KEIL, F.C. (1989) *Concepts, Kinds and Cognitive Development*, MIT Press. A reasonably up-to-date coverage of the development of conceptual cat-egories.

NEISSER, U. (ed.) (1987) *Concepts and Conceptual Development*, Cam-bridge University Press. A useful collection of articles, including contribu-tions by many of the key researchers mentioned in Part I.

BARSALOU, L.W. (1992) *Cognitive Psychology: An Overview for Cogni-tive Scientists*, Lawrence Erlbaum Associates. A general textbook which includes discussion of Barsalou's own work on conceptual categories.

Part II
Object Recognition

Ilona Roth

Contents

1   *Introduction*

Part I of this book discussed the representations responsible for our capacity to mentally group objects, entities and events into categories. Much of the discussion was concerned with mental representations for object categories. As we saw, such representations are well established in memory, furnishing an overall representation of the world as we know it. Part II will focus on the perceptual aspects of object categorization: the fact that a real object with visual features such as four legs, a flat seat, and a vertical back is actually perceived as a chair. It will concentrate on the perceptual processes and representations responsible for this visual **object recognition.**

The importance of understanding object recognition is readily illustrated if you look around the room that you are in now. Without doubt, most of what you see consists of objects. Each of these objects has a particular size, shape, colour and surface texture. You will be aware, not only of the objects themselves, but of their positions in relation to you, to each other and to their background. If asked, you could describe this 'spatial layout' in terms of what objects are ahead and to either side. But even if this knowledge is not verbalized, it is clearly 'there' — if you get up and walk around the room it is not a problem to negotiate your way among the objects without bumping into them.

There is a paradox about this visual awareness: it seems to come to us spontaneously and without effort but it actually consists of a number of remarkable and complex achievements. It would take too long to list all of the achievements which contribute to object recognition, but the discussion in Part II will focus upon some of the more important ones. Part III will consider the special case of recognizing faces.

1.1   *Structure and invariance*

The first achievement is that we see objects at all! That is, our perceptions consist of structured coherent entities, rather than a jumbled mass of edges, surfaces, corners and lines. Though we are not aware of it, our visual systems have to 'decide' which edges, surfaces, corners and so on go together to form units or wholes. This process is known as **perceptual segregation** or **perceptual grouping**. It becomes easier to understand why this is a visual 'problem' when we encounter cases where this process goes wrong. An example is illustrated in Figure 2.1 overleaf.

The goal for a psychological account of visual perception is to explain how the visual system gets this segregation process right — at least most of the time.

Figure 2.1   What is this? If you cannot see what is in the picture, turn to page 81 for the answer

A second achievement is that any given object is recognized as a single three-dimensional (3-D) entity despite the fact that input to the visual system consists of a two-dimensional (2-D) pattern which varies according to the object's position, lighting and the viewpoint from which it is seen. The starting point for vision is that light, reflected from objects, reaches the eyes, which are the sense organs for vision. The light forms an **image** on the **retina** — the layer of light-sensitive nerve cells at the back of the eye — and from this image the visual system constructs an 'interpretation' of the object that it originated from. The image is not in any way a copy of the object — it is just a two-dimensional array of points at which light has stimulated light-sensitive cells. Yet what is seen, on the basis of this image, is in three dimensions. In addition, this perception is stable or invariant though the image is not.

One form of this **perceptual invariance** is **size constancy**. If you move closer to an object, then the size of the image which the object forms on your retina will get larger (see Figure 2.2). The same thing happens when you point a camera at an object you wish to photograph. If you are far away, the image of this object will occupy a small proportion of

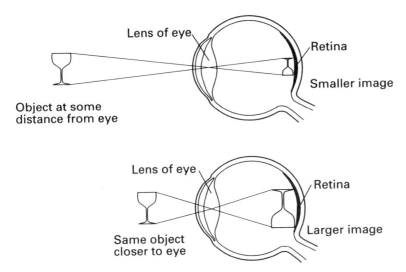

Figure 2.2   Size constancy. The nearer an object is to the eye, the larger the image it forms on the retina. Yet the perceived size of the object does not fluctuate with distance

the total photograph. On the other hand, if you are close to, the object will take up most of the photograph.

The paradox, in the case of human vision (and probably that of other species too), is that the *perceived* size of objects does not fluctuate with changes in their distance from the eye but, within reasonable limits, remains constant or invariant. Size constancy is paralleled in an even more remarkable way by constancy in the perceived colour and shape of objects.

The phenomenon of **shape constancy** is illustrated by Figure 2.3, which shows the same object from two different viewpoints: (a) and

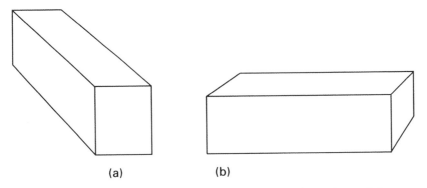

Figure 2.3   Shape constancy. Two quite different viewpoints of the same object do not stop us from recognizing the common source

(b). The pattern of lines, and hence the image which is formed on the retina, is different for these two different viewpoints. The image is said to be **viewpoint dependent** or **viewpoint centred**. Yet the object is recognized as one and the same. In real life, our viewpoint of objects changes all the time (think of the different angles from which you view, say, your cooker, as you move around the kitchen) and yet we do not experience fluctuations in the perceived shape of these objects — if we did we would not recognize them as having a continued identity. Our perceptions of objects are said to be **viewpoint independent** or **object-centred**.

Finally, notice that the information provided by an object, seen from a particular viewpoint, may be partial or incomplete: part of the object may be obscured by deep shadow, or occluded (concealed) by another object. Yet we can still, within limits, see and recognize the object for what it is (see Figure 2.4).

A further goal for a psychological account of perception is to explain how this perceptual invariance comes about. Part II will be particularly concerned with shape. Size constancy is discussed in many more elementary texts, including, for instance, Roth (1990) (see Chapter 10 by Greene). Colour constancy is addressed in a classic paper by Land (1977).

Figure 2.4   We recognize the object despite the bars which occlude part of it

1.2   Recognition and identification

Just as the continued identity of particular objects is recognized despite the fluctuating and incomplete information they provide to the visual system, so *different* objects are recognized as members of the same category, despite differences in their size, shape, colour and so on. As we saw in Part I, a variety of different objects are treated as members of a category such as 'chair'. Part II will consider how this categorization can be carried out on the basis of visual characteristics alone.

Remember that this categorization of objects can be more or less specific. Recognizing that an object is a chair corresponds to Rosch's *basic level* of categorization, as discussed in Part I, and a great deal of object recognition involves categorization at this basic level. But at times our perceptions are more precise: we can *identify* an object as a specific chair (e.g. the chair I use for work, my child's small chair), or as a type of chair (a Chippendale chair, a rocking chair). Perceptual categorizations of this more specific kind are at the subordinate level.

1.3   Using and naming

The perception of our surroundings as a structured stable arrangement of recognizable objects enables us to react appropriately. We can move around without bumping into objects or knocking them over, and, in addition, we can use them appropriately. If I recognize an object as a chair, this tells me that I can sit on it.

Much of the time, recognition permits objects to be named too. But this is not always the case. There are instances where we may recognize an object, even be able to say what it is for, but be unable to produce a name for it. For some unfortunate people who have suffered particular types of brain damage, there is a permanent **dissociation** between the ability to recognize objects visually and to name them. Such individuals may, for instance, be able to describe what an object looks like or what it is for without ever being able to say what it is called. This is one type of evidence that naming is a separable process within object recognition.

1.4   Rapidity and spontaneity

Many of the achievements discussed so far occur rapidly, spontaneously and without any deliberate effort. They also appear to be outside our conscious control: we are unable to choose whether to see things as we do. This **automaticity** is well illustrated by the familiar perceptual illusion shown in Figure 2.5 overleaf.

Figure 2.5 The Müller-Lyer illusion

Even though the two horizontal lines are of the same length, we are unable to choose to see them that way: we automatically perceive the bottom line as longer and no amount of conscious effort can alter this perception, even once we know that it is erroneous.

Perceptual skills which are innate (i.e. dependent on inherited mechanisms) are the ones most likely to be beyond our conscious access or control. These include our perception of colour, of figures which stand out against background, and of depth. Other perceptual skills may become fully or partly automatic as a result of learning.

SAQ 11
Can you think of a perceptual skill which clearly requires deliberate effort in small children, but becomes automatic in adults?

There are also perceptual tasks which require a deliberate effort and are under conscious control. Look, for example, at Figure 2.6. This is taken from a drawing called *Steps* by Josef Albers. You may see this as a flight of steps which starts in the top left-hand corner and recedes into the bottom right-hand corner, or which starts in the bottom right-hand corner and recedes into the top left-hand corner. Whichever way you see it, the perception will probably remain fairly stable, but it is also possible, with some effort and concentration, to reverse the perspective. This kind of alternation is optional and under the control of a conscious strategy. Note too that whereas automatic perceptions occur very rapidly — almost instantaneously it may seem — this type of effortful, controlled perceptual behaviour requires a noticeable amount of time.

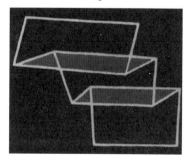

Figure 2.6 Perceptually reversible steps   (from the drawing *Steps* by Josef Albers)

Now that some of the phenomena which perceptual theories and models are designed to explain have been highlighted, we should consider some general theoretical assumptions which are made.

1.5   Theoretical assumptions

As we saw, the information available to the perceptual system is usually partial, fragmentary and fluctuating. Yet our perceptual experience is of structured, coherent objects which we can recognize, use and usually name. This has led most theorists to assume that complex *processes* occur between the retinal image and the final perception.

We also saw that there are a number of *distinct* perceptual achievements — the process of seeing objects as structured coherent wholes is logically separate from the process of recognizing or naming them. This has led theorists to propose that incoming information is processed as a sequence of **stages**, each delivering a different representation and providing the basis for further stages. Some theorists make the further assumption that these stages comprise independent **modules**, each of which is completed without influence from the other modules.

Different theoretical approaches are distinguished by their assumptions about the nature and function of processing stages and about how all these stages are organized with respect to each other. These models have been traditionally classified into two general types. One type of model assumes a sequence of stages which commences with a *low-level analysis* of the retinal image, and builds up gradually to an 'interpretation' based on a comparison with stored knowledge. The underlying assumption is that, though the information in the retinal image is partial and fragmentary, a sequence of processes operating solely on this input will be sufficiently 'clever' to disambiguate the ambiguities and fill in the gaps in this information.

This idea is termed **bottom-up processing** to denote a processing sequence which starts at the input and builds upwards to an interpretation. According to this bottom-up approach, expectations, derived from stored knowledge about what an object might be, play no role in processing the input, until the final stage at which an 'interpretation' is made. For instance, we have, stored in our memories, the information that four vertical legs and a horizontal seat are typical features of chairs. We also know in what type of context chairs are likely to occur. According to bottom-up approaches, this information does not influence the analysis of retinal input. It is accessed only to draw the final conclusion that the object we see is a chair. This mode of processing information is also known as **data-driven processing** because it is guided or driven solely by the sensory data which is available from the input.

Processing which operates bottom-up is also characterized as automatic and outside the organism's conscious control.

Some theorists have argued, however, that since the information in the retinal image is ambiguous or fragmentary, this bottom-up, data-driven processing would be insufficient to permit the perception of objects, scenes, etc. This is seen to be possible only if *stored knowledge* exerts an influence at some stage in the processing of input, providing additional information which helps to resolve the ambiguities or inadequacies in the input, thus permitting suitable interpretations to be made. This type of sequence is described as **top-down processing** and, because it is influenced by stored knowledge, **conceptually-driven processing**. Top-down processing is usually characterized as combining some automatic processing with some which is optional and under the organism's conscious control.

The organization of Part II reflects a bottom-up approach to explaining object recognition; that is, it treats the retinal image as the starting point for perception and considers the processes leading to object recognition as a series of stages which operate in turn on this initial input. However, as these stages become more complex, we will need to consider alternative accounts of how they are organized. Besides evidence which suggests a role for top-down, conceptually-driven processes, there is evidence that treating processing as a series of independent stages, operating one after another, is an oversimplification. Section 7.2 will examine an alternative conceptualization known as a **cascade model** in which a number of processing stages interact with one another.

The next section will outline the main methods used to explore the processing which results in object recognition.

Summary of Section 1

- Visual perception represents a paradox: it has an effortless, spontaneous quality, but actually represents some complex and remarkable achievements.
- We see the world as consisting of structured, stable entities or objects. Individual objects are seen as invariant despite variations in their distance, lighting conditions, and position relative to the observer, all of which cause fluctuations in the information provided to the visual system.
- Objects are recognized as belonging to meaningful categories. Much of object recognition occurs at Rosch's basic level. However, objects may also be individually identified.
- The perceptual achievements of structure, invariance and recognition enable us to react appropriately to objects. Usually, but not invariably, we can name them too.

- Many, but not all, of these perceptual achievements occur automatically and outside our conscious control.
- Traditionally, two broad approaches to object recognition have been distinguished: bottom-up, data-driven models assume that object recognition commences with analysis of the information in the retinal image, and builds up stage-by-stage into an interpretation of an object. Top-down, conceptually-driven models assume that information stored in memory influences the processing of retinal information at one or more stages. An alternative type of model — a cascade model — emphasizes the interaction of successive processing stages.

(Figure 2.1 shows a Dalmatian dog sniffing among fallen leaves.)

2   Studying visual perception

What methods are appropriate to studying and explaining a set of phenomena which combine, in a most intriguing and elusive way, apparent simplicity with underlying complexity? The methods used to study both object recognition (Part II) and face recognition (Part III) are more diverse and more specialized than those we encountered in Part I. They are set out in detail here.

2.1   Artificial intelligence

The term **artificial intelligence** covers a *range* of approaches which involve designing computer systems to carry out perceptual tasks such as seeing and recognizing objects. The nature of artificial-intelligence approaches varies according to the goal to be achieved. For instance, some approaches have the goal of a solution to a particular practical problem, such as the design of a robot in a car factory that can identify objects on the assembly line, or, in medical diagnosis, a computer that can 'see' defective cells in a blood sample. Other approaches have the quite different goal of *simulating* the workings of a biological visual system in an artificial or computer system. The idea here is to build a machine which will work in the same way as the biological visual system.

However, for present purposes, the most relevant artificial intelligence approach is a third, which has neither the practical goal of developing a 'seeing' robot, nor the goal of 'mimicking' a specific visual system. Instead, this third approach seeks to establish a general theory of how vision works; that is, to elucidate the general design principles of any vision system whether artificial or biological. An important contribution in this area has come from the work of Marr (1982). Part of his contribution consists of a **metatheory**: an overall framework specifying how the task of investigating visual perception should proceed. This metatheory comprises three distinct levels of analysis:

1 **The computational theory level**

This is concerned with a theoretical analysis of the tasks which perception accomplishes and the methods needed to accomplish them.

2 **The algorithmic level**

This is concerned with identifying the actual operations by which perceptual tasks are accomplished — processes and representations in a biological visual system, and **algorithms** in a computer.

3 **The hardware level**

This is concerned with the mechanisms underlying the operations of the system — **neuronal** or nervous system structures in a biological vision system, and electronic components in a computer.

Using this general strategy, Marr developed his own specific proposals about how vision works, and his work will be referred to at various points in Part II. Most of this work is couched at the first and second of his three levels of analysis: like many artificial intelligence (AI) researchers in the 1980s, Marr saw the third level as subsidiary, arguing that it is in principle possible for different types of computer hardware to subserve the same programs or 'software'. More recent AI work has had the specific aim of integrating the general principles at computational, algorithmic and hardware levels.

The main advantage of the AI approach is that the researcher needs to be absolutely explicit about the principles involved: otherwise the system will not perform the designated task. This means that any system which is constructed is necessarily fully understood by the person who has built it.

However, there is a problem in evaluating the evidence which comes from artificial vision systems. Suppose we were trying to program a computer to 'see' a chair in a room. How would we decide whether the computer had 'seen' the chair? We know whether a person can see the chair because she can say what she is seeing or provide a written description of it. She can also answer questions such as 'Is what you see a chair or a table?' She can sit down on the chair, walk around it, or push it up to a table. We can use all of these responses or 'outputs' as criteria of seeing. The criteria of computer vision are invariably more limited than this. A system may be said to 'see' if it can produce a description of an object, but this does not necessarily mean it can walk round the object or use it appropriately. This is one of the things which makes it difficult to compare the results of AI approaches directly with models of human object recognition.

2.2   *Perceptual demonstrations and experiments*

The most traditional method of studying visual perception consists of **perceptual demonstrations**: presenting human subjects with simple (usually two-dimensional) figures and asking them what they see. This method requires that the subjects report their **introspections**, and it has yielded important information about the overall nature of the task which the visual system has to accomplish — Marr's first level of analysis. Examples of figures used in perceptual demonstrations are Figures 2.1, 2.5 and 2.6. All of these draw attention to the inherently ambiguous and impoverished nature of perceptual input, and point to the need for theories which explain the visual system's supreme capacity to make sense of this input.

However, perceptual demonstrations pose two problems as a method for investigating visual perception. First, while they highlight the nature of the phenomena to be explained, they do not in themselves explain them. Secondly, introspections are potentially unreliable: reports may vary from one individual to another, and there is no way of checking whether any individual's report is an accurate reflection of what the person is perceiving. Many people therefore favour **experiments** as a way of addressing these two problems.

Experiments involve studying subjects' responses to carefully selected types of visual information presented under carefully controlled conditions. Various techniques are employed to measure subjects' responses to systematic variations in stimulus characteristics. Conclusions are usually based on the average response of a sizeable group of subjects, rather than on the idiosyncratic responses of individual subjects.

Most contemporary experiments employ stimuli which are **naturalistic**, in the sense that they consist of relatively complex shapes or patterns like those encountered in the real world. Subjects are asked to respond to such stimuli (e.g. by naming them, categorizing them, or matching one with another). The main measures of their response are reaction times and errors: by comparing reaction times and accuracy for different stimuli under different task conditions, inferences can be drawn about the underlying perceptual processes. The insights derived are primarily at Marr's second level of analysis: the algorithmic level.

2.3   *Neuropsychology and neurophysiology*

Neuropsychology typically involves drawing inferences about the mechanisms of normal perception from an analysis of which perceptual abilities are lost when an individual suffers accidental injury or **lesion** to the brain. The underlying assumption is that the deficits in a damaged visual system highlight how the intact visual system works.

It should not be thought that neuropsychology permits straightfor-ward identification of which areas of the brain are responsible for which types of perceptual ability. Such localization of function is possible only at a fairly gross level. For instance, lesions in an area of the brain called the **occipital lobes** tend to be associated with loss of the ability to deal with specific visual dimensions such as colour or depth, whereas lesions in other 'visual' areas of the brain produce loss of more com-plex visual abilities such as object recognition or naming. Since the anatomical position of the occipital lobes means that they receive retinal input before it reaches other brain areas, it seems reasonable to con-clude that this area has a role in the early stages of visual information processing.

One problem with such attempts to localize function is that patients with lesions in different brain areas sometimes display loss of the same functions. This may be because more than one brain site has a role in the same visual ability. Another problem is that lesions may have the effect of interfering with the pathways between one brain area and another, rather than 'knocking out' an area *per se*. In both these cases, loss of visual function would not permit inferences about which brain areas are normally involved.

Much contemporary neuropsychology is concerned less with local-ization of function and more with identifying the different systems which contribute to visual processing, the extent to which they are function-ally independent of each other, and the extent to which they interact. A key concept in this approach is **dissociation**. Simple dissociation refers to the loss of a single visual ability (e.g. the ability to name objects, after brain injury). Simple dissociation is not always informa-tive: if the visual skill happens to be a particularly complex one, it may simply be the first to be affected by trauma to the brain. Much more informative are **double dissociations** in which patient A displays loss of one visual ability (say recognizing an object from a picture) while retaining a second ability intact (say recognizing an object from a verbal description); patient B displays the opposite pattern. These selective deficits cannot be due to brain trauma 'knocking out' the most diffi-cult visual abilities. The strong implication from such selective impair-ments is that the two abilities rely on functionally separable systems or processes.

Notice that neuropsychology is complementary to, rather than a substitute for, experiments: the means used to establish a patient's visual impairments are frequently experimental.

SAQ 12
Which of Marr's levels of analysis do you think are informed by neuropsychological studies?

Neurophysiology shares with neuropsychology a focus on the neural mechanisms and processes of the brain and nervous system. But whereas neuropsychology uses evidence drawn from fairly gross, accidental damage to these mechanisms, neurophysiology employs special techniques to explore, in detail, how the intact mechanisms work. The most important method involves inserting microscopic electrodes into single cells in the visual system of cats or monkeys in order to measure how these cells respond when particular types of visual stimuli are presented to the organism. The general insight gained from this work is that cells in different parts of the visual system display *selective* responses to different stimulus characteristics, being selectively responsive to orientation, colour, movement and even shape. This information has guided hypotheses about the organization of information processing in object recognition, and particularly about the extent to which different stimulus dimensions are processed by separate modules. Neurophysiology thus informs two of Marr's levels: the algorithmic and the hardware levels.

Summary of Section 2

- The main methods used to investigate object recognition are artificial intelligence, perceptual demonstrations, experiments, neuropsychology, and neurophysiology.
- Artificial intelligence involves designing computer systems to carry out perceptual tasks such as seeing and recognizing objects. Much of this work seeks to elucidate the general design principles of a visual system, whether artificial or biological.
- Perceptual demonstrations involve presenting human subjects with simple figures and asking them to describe what they see. They have highlighted the capacity of the visual system to deal with impoverished and ambiguous input.
- Experiments are used to study responses to visual stimuli presented under controlled conditions. Reaction time experiments are used to draw inferences about how visual information is processed, from the speed and accuracy with which subjects respond.
- Neuropsychology involves drawing inferences about the mechanisms and systems of normal perception from an analysis of the perceptual deficits which occur after brain damage. The double disassociation is the most useful pattern of deficits for such inferences.
- Neurophysiology employs special recording techniques to study intact visual mechanisms in non-human animals.
- Marr's metatheory identifies three levels of analysis as necessary to understanding how visual perception works: the computational theory level, the algorithmic level, and the hardware level.

- The nature of these levels and the way in which the research methods discussed in this section relate to them are shown in Table 2.1.

Table 2.1

Marr's level of analysis	Type of analysis	Type of explanation	Methods used
1 Computational theory	What functions does perception achieve?	A general theory of how inputs in the form of images are transformed into descriptions of objects, events, etc., which provide a basis for action	Computational (AI); perceptual demonstrations
2 Algorithmic	What are the operations which achieve these functions?	Processes and representations in a biological visual system; algorithms in a computer	Computational (AI); experimental; neuropsychological
3 Hardware	What are the mechanisms underlying these operations?	Neuronal mechanisms of human vision or electronic components of computer	Computational (AI); neuropsychological; neurophysiological

3   Early stages: image processing

We shall now begin to consider the processes by which we see and recognize objects such as chairs in a room, taking Marr's proposals about these processes as a starting point. Marr's approach is strictly bottom-up: it starts with the input to the perceptual system in the form of the retinal image and describes the *stages* in the processing of this image. Each stage takes as its input the information from the previous stage and transforms it into a more complex description or *representation* of the input, couched in terms of basic elements or **primitives** which are specific to that stage.

You may find the way in which these proposals are presented unfamiliar. Ideas based on the methods of experimentation, neuropsychology and neurophysiology are usually presented in the form of theories or models capable of generating hypotheses testable against empirical evidence. In contrast, the AI work of people like Marr is presented as a theoretical analysis of solutions to the problems which must be solved in visual object recognition, together with a description of the actual algorithms which implement the solution (the algorithmic level). It is this **implementation** which constitutes the empirical test in AI models — if the system actually runs, it shows that the proposals are a viable (though not necessarily correct) account of how vision works. Notice, however, that parts of Marr's system exist only in the form of theoretical proposals — they have never actually been implemented.

3.1   Overview of Marr's model

In Marr's model, the process of vision is seen to begin when light rays from objects or scenes in the real world are focused on to a light-sensitive surface (screen or retina) forming an image. The stages which operate in turn on this image are as follows:

1 *Grey level description*
  This initial stage consists of measuring the intensity of light at each point in the image, generating the so called **grey level description**.

2 *Primal sketch*
  There are two main modules within this stage. The first is concerned with deriving from the grey level description a description of potentially significant regions; that is, those which may correspond, in the real world, to the edges of objects, the boundaries between overlapping objects, and the texture of objects. This description is known as the **raw primal sketch**. The subsequent early visual processing module is concerned with providing information about how these regions 'go together' to form structures (i.e. it generates a description corresponding to the outline shapes of the objects present in the real world scene). This description is known as the **full primal sketch**.

  All descriptions at this stage of processing are specific to the particular location or viewpoint from which the scene giving rise to the image is viewed. As we saw in Section 1, the final outcome of object recognition is a perception which is invariant across different viewpoints. However, at this early stage of visual processing, the descriptions which are extracted from the image change as the viewpoint changes. These descriptions, then, are not invariant but are said to be *viewpoint dependent*.

3 *2.5D sketch*
  The **2.5D sketch** is a representation of how the surfaces in the scene from which the image derives relate to one another and to the person

(or computer) viewing them. Descriptions at this stage are not in-variant but are still viewpoint dependent. The layout of surfaces, viewed from a different angle, would evoke a different description.

4 *Object recognition*

The modules at this stage are concerned with extracting descriptions of the appearance of objects in a scene, such that they can be recognized or identified. In order for this to happen, the viewpoint-dependent descriptions from the earlier stages must be converted into descriptions which are *independent of viewpoint*: so-called *object-centred* descriptions.

The stages in Marr's model are shown in Figure 2.7.

The remainder of Section 3 will be concerned with the derivation of the grey level description and the raw primal sketch. The raw primal sketch consists of primitives, including **edge segments**, which signify regions of potential significance in the image. Almost all theories of perception assume an initial stage in which information about edges is extracted from the input and, as we shall see, there is neurophysiological evidence for such a stage in biological vision systems.

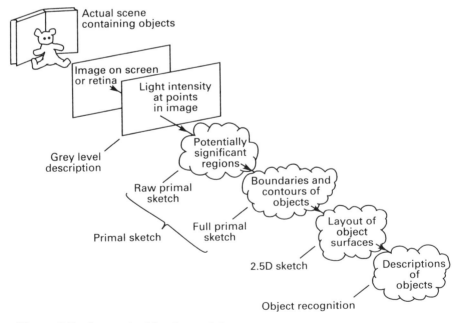

Figure 2.7   Stages in Marr's model

3.2   Generating a grey level description

As we have seen, the very first operation is to measure the intensity of light at every point in the incoming image. These intensities correspond in turn to the amounts of light reflected or emitted by the surfaces of objects. (For simplicity, only monochromatic static images will be considered here, although in a system approaching the complexity of a natural vision system, the intensity of wavelength (colour) information and fluctuations in intensity with movement would have to be taken into account.) The light-sensitive surface on to which the input is focused gives a measured response, depending on light intensity, at every point where the light strikes it (see Figure 2.8b overleaf). This pattern of varying light intensities is represented, point by point, by a 2-D array of numbers known individually as **pixels** (see Figure 2.8c).

The reason the whole array is called a *grey level description* is that, for monochromatic images, each pixel number represents the intensity of light at that point on a scale of 'greyness' running from black through greys to white.

SAQ 13
Draw circles around the numbers representing the highest and lowest intensity points in the inset box within Figure 2.8c.

The 2-D array of pixels shown in Figure 2.8 very probably has its equivalent in the 2-D array of **receptors** (rods and cones) which constitute the retina in biological visual systems. Each receptor cell responds to light by a change in the voltage difference across its membrane or cell wall. The size of this change or **depolarization** depends on the intensity of the light reaching the cell. Thus, the overall pattern of these depolarizations serves, like the grey level description, to code, point by point, the pattern of light intensity in the input.

3.3   Computing image intensity changes

The next main task for the vision system is to compute or calculate the *intensity changes* that exist from one point of an image to another. What this means is putting together the point-by-point intensity information in the grey level description into an overall representation of how intensity varies across the entire image.

In the real world, changes in the intensity of reflected light arise at the boundaries and contours of objects (i.e. at edges which may be significant in defining an object's overall shape). However, the edges around and within an object are not the only places where light intensity changes arise. Figure 2.9 (see page 91) shows a picture in which the light intensity changes along a single line, drawn at eye-level, have been measured and plotted graphically.

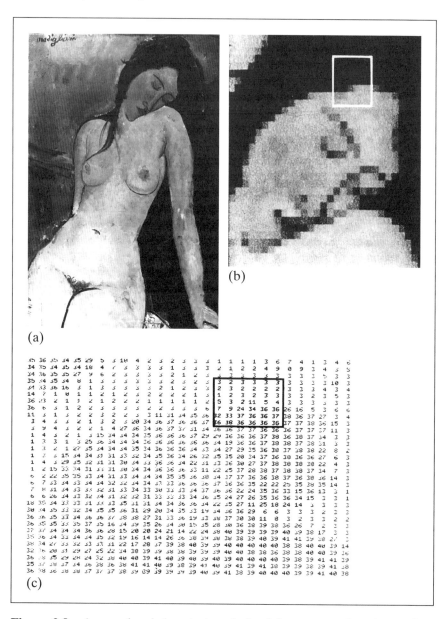

Figure 2.8   A grey level description derived from part of a picture (*Female Nude* by Amedeo Modigliani): (a) The original picture; (b) A computerized image of the face from the picture, showing the variations in greyness across the image; (c) The grey level description of this image, with an inset box corresponding to the inset on the image (high numbers in this array represent pixels of high intensity, low numbers pixels of low intensity)   (based on Frisby, 1979, Figure 2)

Figure 2.9   The rising and falling line indicates changes in the intensity of light reflected by the picture at points along the straight line at eye-level. The larger and steeper the rise or fall, the larger the change in intensity (Mark Georgeson, University of Aston)

SAQ 14
Using the graph in Figure 2.9, mark with a pencil where on the line the largest changes in intensity arise (i.e. those which are both steep and deep). Now work out whether these large-scale intensity changes correspond to edges of important features of the object. Apart from these intensity changes, is the level of intensity along the line constant?

As you will have found, there are three types of intensity change along the line:
1 Large-scale changes which correspond to edges of the object and to the contours of features within it (e.g. the edge of the hairline, the eye-socket).
2 Relatively large-scale changes which correspond to changes in the surface texture of the object, the boundaries of shadows, etc.
3 Small-scale fluctuations which correspond to nothing of any significance in the object. These are due to random fluctuations in the amount of light reflected from one point to another.

It should be clear that if a computer is to come up with a description which provides significant information about the edges and contours of an object, it needs to distinguish between the three types of intensity change listed above. In practice, this is accomplished in stages. Within the raw primal sketch stage, algorithms operate to filter out the *third* kind of intensity change. The *second* kind of intensity change is treated as potentially significant and is included in the raw primal sketch stage. It is only at the full primal sketch stage that algorithms can operate to distinguish between intensity changes (1) and (2) in order to produce a description of the edges and internal contours of an object. The processes which, by serving to filter out the third kind of intensity change, result in the raw primal sketch, will now be described.

3.4   Generating the raw primal sketch

The general procedure adopted by the vision system to filter out random intensity fluctuations is known as **smoothing**. Smoothing involves replacing the intensity value of each pixel element in the grey level description by the average value of it and its neighbours. This has the effect of 'playing down' or attenuating those intensity changes which are random, and accentuating or sharpening up those which are potentially significant.

The general effect of this smoothing operation is to 'blur' the detail in the input, while leaving potentially significant contours apparent. The problem is to set the level of averaging, and thus blurring, appropriately in order to capture *only* the potentially significant regions of intensity change. As it turns out, there is no *single* level which will do this, because the appropriate level depends on the particular object which has given rise to the input. For some objects, quite gradual changes in the intensity of light they reflect are actually significant — they correspond to contours, boundaries, etc. — whereas for others they do not. But the vision system does not 'know' this in advance, and therefore does not have a single criterion level of intensity change to work with.

The solution is that several different levels of smoothing are applied simultaneously to the grey level description, producing multiple representations, each blurred to a different extent (see Figure 2.10a overleaf). Each of the multiple blurred representations is now transformed into a new representation using primitives called **zero crossings**. The value of each zero crossing indicates how sharply or steeply intensity rises and falls at a particular location in the image. Zero crossings derived from very blurred representations give this gradient information only for the most significant intensity changes, but they do so at the expense of precise information about the locations of these changes in the image. The opposite is true of zero crossings from slightly blurred representations. (See Figure 2.10b.) Marr's algorithm combines the information from these different sources in such a way as to maximize the information about *both* the location and scale of significant intensity changes.

Finally, using the zero crossings, four different kinds of intensity changes are represented as primitives in the raw primal sketch. Three of these, **blobs, edge segments,** and **bars**, are shown in Figure 2.10c. Some of these, particularly edge segments, will be 'put together' in the full primal sketch to derive information about the boundaries and contours of objects. But others, such as blobs, may be used to locate regions of texture change in objects.

3.5   *The resolution of ambiguity in the raw primal sketch*

In Section 3, we have looked in detail at just one module from Marr's model — further modules, which we will touch on later, use the primitives of the raw primal sketch to generate increasingly complex representations of the input, leading ultimately to an interpretation. However, even this early stage will serve to illustrate the general approach, within this model, to resolving the ambiguities and inadequacies of the retinal image.

The key point is that the model assumes a bottom-up system in which the processing stages have no access to knowledge about the possible identity of the objects it is viewing. Instead, the algorithms which operate on the input incorporate general principles about which kinds of information in the input are likely to be significant, in the sense that they are likely to correspond to those characteristics of any object which might be useful in identifying it. Small, local intensity

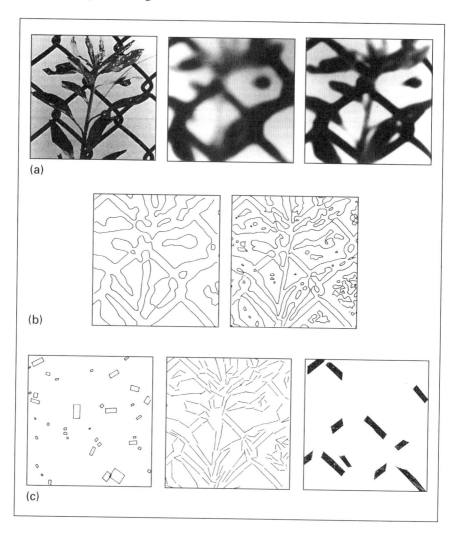

Figure 2.10 Smoothing of images and raw primal sketch primitives: (a) The different degrees of blurring (centre and right) which result when two different levels of smoothing are applied to the original image shown at the left; (b) Two different zero crossings. The left-hand zero crossing comes from a more blurred image. It includes only the most important intensity change information, but information about location is lost. The right-hand zero crossing comes from a less blurred image and incorporates some of the less significant intensity change information. However, location is clearly shown; (c) The blobs, edge segments and bars which result from combining zero crossings (based on Marr and Hildreth, 1980, Figures 1 and 8)

changes in the input do not normally correspond to anything significant in their source objects and this is why the smoothing algorithm of the raw primal sketch filters them out, leaving only the larger scale intensity changes in play.

In Marr's terminology, the algorithm makes an **assertion** that the large-scale intensity changes are going to be the significant ones. However, as we saw, some ambiguity is left in play at the raw primal sketch stage, since this stage does not differentiate between those large-scale image intensity changes corresponding to edges and contours, and those which correspond to surface texture changes and shadow boundaries. It is the role of the subsequent module — the full primal sketch — to select those larger scale intensity changes which signify the edges and contours of objects. This is again achieved by assertions guided by general principles about the way the intensity of reflected light fluctuates in the areas of significant features of objects. At each subsequent stage in Marr's model, a new representation of input is formed in which some ambiguities are resolved, and others are kept in play, to be resolved at a later stage. Only at the final stage of object identification are all the ambiguities resolved in what are hoped to be correct assertions about the identity of the object(s) being looked at.

An important question is whether this model is plausible as an account of how objects are seen and recognized. It would be premature to attempt to evaluate the model as a whole since its later stages have not been discussed. However, we can evaluate Marr's claims about the early stages of vision.

3.6   Evaluation

The first question is whether Marr's model 'works': that is, does it generate a symbolic representation which corresponds to the significant components of the input? The algorithms were implemented by Marr and Hildreth (1980) and broadly speaking they meet this criterion. Figure 2.11 overleaf shows raw primal sketch descriptions of some of the objects and patterned surfaces analysed by Marr's program.

However, the fact that the program works does not mean that biological vision systems work in the same way. The main evidence supporting the relevance of Marr's model to biological vision comes from classic neurophysiological studies concerning the responses to light stimuli of single cells in the retina and visual cortex of cats and monkeys. The responses appear to mirror Marr's algorithm in achieving the optimal compromise between signalling the location of intensity changes in the image and signalling how sharp these intensity changes are. These responses thus give information about the likely position of edges and contours in the input.

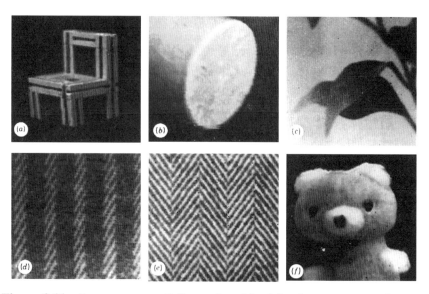

Figure 2.11   Images successfully analysed by Marr's program to the raw primal sketch stage: (a) a chair; (b) a rod; (c) a plant; (d and e) patterned surfaces; (f) a teddy bear   (Marr, 1976, Figure 4)

Despite this 'parallel', Marr and Hildreth's is not the only algorithm which has been devised as a means of generating the raw primal sketch. Other more recent algorithms have been tested against the data from human perceptual experiments with, it is claimed, a better fit than Marr and Hildreth's. If you wish to read more about this work, you should consult Bruce and Green (1990). Though the nature of the algorithm which provides the 'best fit' with biological vision is controversial, the general claim, that the early stage of vision consists of a representation of simple components such as edge segments, is accepted.

Summary of Section 3

- Marr's image-processing model describes visual perception as a bottom-up sequence of independent stages, each stage operating on the input from the previous stage to generate a more complex representation.
- In Marr's model the process of vision is assumed to commence with the formation of an image on a light-sensitive surface (retina or computer screen). This is converted into a grey level description which represents the light intensities at individual points in the image.
- The goal of Marr's primal sketch stage is to convert the grey level description into a representation of those light intensity changes which correspond to edges and contours in the objects from which they

derive. This is accomplished in two substages or modules: the raw primal sketch and the full primal sketch.

- Within the raw primal sketch an algorithm operates to 'smooth' the intensity changes in the input, thus accentuating regions of maximum intensity change. Multiple representations, smoothed or blurred to different extents are produced.
- The locations of points of maximum intensity change are represented as 'zero crossings'. The zero crossing information from the multiple blurred images is put together to generate the edge segments and other primitives of the raw primal sketch.
- In Marr's model, the ambiguity of the input is resolved by algorithmic 'assertions' informed by general principles about what aspects of input are likely to correspond to significant characteristics of objects.
- A parallel for Marr's algorithm is found in the response characteristics of single cells in biological vision systems.

4   Intermediate stages: grouping the components

The claim made in Section 3 was that the representation initially devised from the retinal image consists of simple components such as the edge segments, blobs, bars and terminations of the raw primal sketch. Yet we perceive the world as made up of structured coherent objects, clearly distinguished from backgrounds, rather than as an uncoordinated mass of fragments. In most bottom-up models, perceptual processes are assumed to operate to 'assemble' these simple components into groupings which begin to reflect the structure of objects. In Marr's model, this process results in the full primal sketch. The initial focus in this section, however, will be on evidence which has come from the perceptual demonstrations of the Gestalt psychologists in the 1920s, and from more recent experimental work.

4.1   Gestalt laws

The best known insight provided by the Gestalt psychologists was that two-dimensional figures (and by implication three-dimensional objects) have properties not found in the component parts — so-called **emergent properties**. On account of this claim, they considered **perceptual grouping** into whole structures to be *the* basic and primary phenomenon of perception. However, contemporary accounts reinterpret perceptual grouping as a stage which operates on simpler elements such as edge segments, initially extracted from the retinal image.

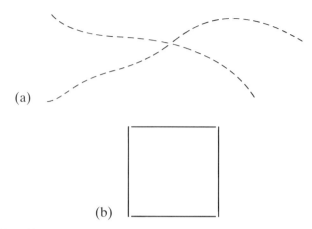

(a)

(b)

Figure 2.12   Illustration of the Gestalt laws of proximity, similarity, good continuity and closure: (a) Proximity, similarity and good continuity all contribute to our seeing this as two lines crossing each other; (b) Closure results in our seeing a square, although there are gaps at the corners

The relevant aspect of the Gestaltists' work is a set of laws describing what types of perceptual structures are systematically evoked by particular types of pattern. Figures 2.12a and 2.12b illustrate some of these laws.

First, in Figure 2.12a the dots are seen as lines, rather than unconnected points, because they are close to one another and similar to one another — illustrating the **law of proximity** and **the law of similarity**. Secondly, these lines are seen as two smooth curves crossing in the middle, rather than as two 'Vs' meeting at a point. This is because it is the former structure which preserves smooth continuity rather than yielding an abrupt change, illustrating the **law of good continuity**. Figure 2.12b is seen as a square even though there are actually gaps in the contour. This illustrates the **law of closure**. Individual laws such as these were held by the Gestalt psychologists to be manifestations of a more basic **Law of Prägnanz**, which Koffka (1935) described as follows: 'Of several geometrically possible organizations, that one will actually occur which possesses the best, simplest and most stable shape.'

SAQ 15
The pattern shown in Figure 2.13 might be structured in each of the following ways:
(a) A square.
(b) A cross.
(c) A triangle plus dot.
Which of these structures do you think conforms to the Law of Prägnanz? Was this how you actually saw the figure?

•   •

•   •

Figure 2.13

The main legacy of the Gestalt movement has been a thorough (and largely accurate) *description* of the set of rules governing how the elements or parts of figures (and by implication 3-D objects) are 'put together' resulting in the perceived segregation of structures from their background and from one another. But the Gestalt psychologists did not have the means to follow up these basic laws with experimental or computational investigations. The method available to them relied upon the introspective reports of their subjects: what has been termed the 'look at the figure and see for yourself' method.

This left the Gestalt psychologists ill-equipped to answer two important questions:

1 *What is the function of Gestalt phenomena?*
   This is a question at Marr's *computational theory* level. It requires an analysis of the overall *role* played by Gestalt grouping processes in delivering to the visual system information which can be used in the perception and recognition of objects and scenes.
2 *How are the laws implemented?*
   This is a question about the *algorithms* or processes which are responsible for producing Gestalt phenomena.

Both of these questions have begun to be addressed by modern experimental and AI work. Sections 4.2 and 4.3 will consider recent work carried out within these two paradigms.

4.2   *Experimental studies of Gestalt grouping phenomena*

Pomerantz (1985) reviewed a number of experiments which provide objective evidence of the effects of Gestalt grouping phenomena on behaviour. This has elucidated a possible role for such grouping in object recognition. Pomerantz argued that if a set of elements lend themselves to perceptual grouping, subjects should have difficulty in responding to one element of the set while ignoring others. Conversely, if a set of elements do not lend themselves to grouping, it should be easy to respond to one member of the set while ignoring others. The objective measure of the extent of grouping was how quickly subjects

TECHNIQUES BOX J

An Experimental Study of Perceptual Grouping
(Pomerantz and Garner, 1973)

Rationale   To demonstrate that if a set of elements are perceived as a perceptual group, it is difficult to classify one element while ignoring the others. Thus, reaction times to deal with one element from a 'groupable' set will be slower than when dealing with one element from a 'non-groupable' set.

Method   Subjects were given a pile of cards, each with a pair of brackets printed on it — see Figure 2.14 for examples. Subjects were asked to sort the cards into two piles (A and B) according to whether the left-hand bracket on each card looks like this '(' or like this ')'. Subjects were told to ignore the right-hand bracket completely in carrying out the task. In one condition the pairs of elements were predicted to be *groupable* whereas in the other they were predicted to be *non-groupable*. In each condition, there was an experimental and a control pack. Figure 2.14 shows examples of groupable and non-groupable elements from both experimental and control packs. The right-hand column summarizes the predictions for each condition.

		Sort into pile A B B A	Predictions
Groupable stimuli	Control	[((] [) (] [) (] [((]	Subjects will group these stimuli, therefore they will have difficulty ignoring the right-hand bracket. Sorting speed for control pack will be relatively unaffected since right-hand bracket always stays the same, but sorting speed for experimental pack will be slow since right-hand bracket varies.
	Experimental	[((] [) (] [))] [( )]	
Non-groupable stimuli	Control	[(⌒] [)⌒] [)⌒] [(⌒]	Subjects will not group these elements, therefore they will ignore right-hand bracket in sorting cards. Thus, no difference in sorting speed between control condition (right-hand bracket constant) and experimental condition (right-hand bracket varies).
	Experimental	[(⌒] [)⌒] [)⌣] [(⌣]	

Figure 2.14

Results   As predicted, when cards had 'groupable' elements on them, subjects were slow in sorting the experimental pack, implying that they were unable to ignore the variations in the irrelevant right-hand brackets. When cards had non-groupable elements there was no difference in the times taken to sort experimental and control packs, implying that subjects were able to ignore variations in the irrelevant right-hand bracket.

could sort or classify one element presented with others which the subject must try to ignore (see Techniques Box J).

The implication of this study is that elements which meet the Gestalt requirements for perceptual grouping (e.g. they are similar to one another, close to one another, etc.) are actually processed differently from elements which do not meet these requirements. In the experimental task, subjects' responses to these groupable elements were inefficient (i.e. slow) because they were trying to select out just one element from the group. By implication, the elements had been effectively grouped together rendering such separation difficult.

What purpose might be served by the processing of elements as coherent, difficult-to-separate groups? Components of input which are *near* to each other, *similar* to each other, or follow each other in a straight line are likely to signify parts of the same object. There is said to be a **non-accidental** correspondence between the components of real objects, and the way their representations are organized in visual input. Hence, the visual system appears to be automatically 'tuned' to assemble those elements of input which are likely to signify parts of the same object. As we shall now see, this theory of the role of Gestalt grouping phenomena is adopted and implemented within Marr's model in order to generate the full primal sketch.

4.3   Computing the full primal sketch: Marr's model

We saw in Section 3 that the output to the raw primal sketch stage was a representation of the potentially significant intensity changes in the image in terms of four types or primitives: edge segments, terminations, blobs and bars. Marr's full primal sketch stage employs the Gestalt principles of proximity, similarity, continuity and closure to group some of these primitives into regions corresponding to the overall outline structure of objects — what is known as the **occluding contour**, as well as the presence of significant component structures within this contour. For instance, if the 'input' to the visual system comes from a human face, the 'output' at the full primal sketch stage would consist of an occluding contour corresponding to the overall outline of the face, together with outlines of significant component regions such as the eyes, nose and mouth.

The use of Gestalt principles occurs not as a single unified stage, but as a series of repeated sub-stages designed to assemble small regions into increasingly large regions. The broad principle guiding this 'assembly' is the **principle of explicit naming**: in order to manipulate a 'thing', or describe 'it', or reason about 'it', the computer begins by giving 'it' a name. The names in question here would be 'regions', 'lines', etc. Figure 2.15 overleaf illustrates the principle at work.

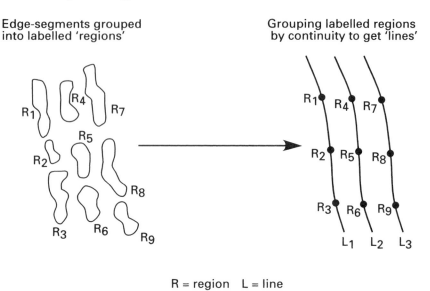

Edge-segments grouped into labelled 'regions'

Grouping labelled regions by continuity to get 'lines'

R = region   L = line

Figure 2.15   The results of grouping of edge segments by the principle of explicit naming to form 'regions' and 'lines'

Various edge segments have been grouped together because they display proximity, figural continuity, and closure: the resulting 'things' are called 'regions'. The symbol 'R' serves as a label or **place token** which asserts that a region has been found at a given location. The 'R' symbols (regions) are then grouped together in turn, because they satisfy the grouping principle of continuity. These then form a new set of assertions, which the computer labels with the place token 'L' for 'lines'.

The importance of the principle of explicit naming is that, once a name or label has been given to an entity derived from the image, the named entity can be used in repeated applications of Gestalt grouping operations to arrive at larger and larger entities.

4.4   The resolution of ambiguity in the full primal sketch

The resolution of ambiguity at this stage of Marr's model is governed by the same general principle which applied at the raw primal sketch stage: the computer only commits itself to those assertions about the characteristics of the input for which the evidence is absolutely clear. In the case of the full primal sketch, the use of grouping rules to make assertions about 'what goes with what' is subject to the strict demand that the configurations provide a good fit: 'near' elements must be near enough, similar elements must be similar enough, and so on. If the fit is not good, the ambiguity is left unresolved (the system remains 'uncommitted' to any grouping). As competing possibilities are gradually taken out by the strict application of such grouping rules, so it becomes possible to employ less stringent demands safely for the remaining points. In short, grouping rules are applied in a manner which resolves ambiguity gradually by progressively reducing the similarity demanded as the computation proceeds.

Marr's model, in keeping with the experimental work of Pomerantz and others, sees Gestalt phenomena as playing a role at an early stage in visual processing, when the main ambiguities about 'what goes with what' in the input are resolved. This resolution of ambiguity is strictly bottom-up: it is not guided by top-down knowledge about what the objects are likely to be. In other words, the system does not group together those points which correspond to the edges of a chair leg because it has hypothesized that the object is a chair: the grouping principles merely reflect general properties of the world.

How far does this bottom-up resolution of ambiguity 'work' (i.e. does it produce 'correct' assertions about 'what goes with what' in the input)? An example of a successful implementation of Marr's full primal sketch stage is shown in Figure 2.16 overleaf.

Figure 2.16 shows the results of implementing the grey level description (b), raw primal sketch (c), and full primal sketch (d, e and f) on an image consisting of a teddy bear (a). Figure 2.16c shows the primitives which result at the raw primal sketch stage. Figure 2.16 (d, e and f) show the result of joining edge segments into regions — they correspond, correctly, to the overall outline (d) as well as to the position of eyes and nose (e) and muzzle (f).

However, this bottom-up application of grouping principles is not always successful. Figure 2.17 (see page 105) shows what happens when the image consists of two overlapping leaves. Remember that the computer does not *know* what the structures are. The application of grouping principles leads to the incorrect assertion that the edge segments derived at the raw primal sketch stage should be joined to produce one structure at the full primal sketch stage. The only way in which Marr's program can avoid an incorrect assertion of this kind is by giving it 'top-down' knowledge about the separate identity of the two leaves.

This does not necessarily imply that natural vision requires an input of top-down knowledge in order to achieve correct grouping at the full primal sketch stage. Two sources of information are available to a natural vision system, which Marr's program does not have. First of all, a natural vision system will move relative to objects it is looking at. In the course of moving, the pattern of input to the retina from, say, overlapping leaves will change in systematic ways which furnish **cues** that they are indeed overlapping, rather than part of the same object.

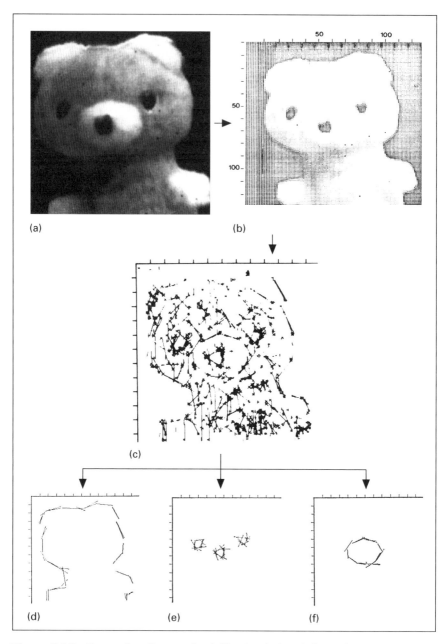

Figure 2.16   Stages leading to the full primal sketch in an implementation of Marr's program: (a) image of teddy bear; (b) grey level description; (c) primitives which result at raw primal sketch stage; (d) overall outline; (e) position of eyes and nose; (f) outline of muzzle   (based on Marr, 1976, Figure 21)

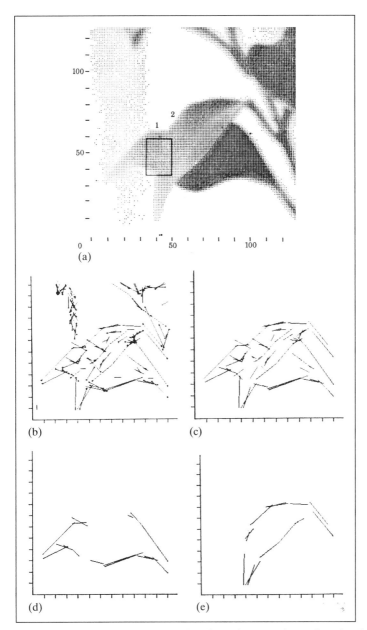

Figure 2.17   Full primal sketch resulting from image of overlapping leaves. The grouping procedures fail to separate the two leaves in (a). Instead, the raw primal sketch (b) evokes the main assertion of a single structure (c). Given top-down knowledge that adjacent segments of the image signify separate objects, the program correctly 'finds' (d) and (e)   (based on Marr, 1976, Figure 13)

In addition, the natural vision system has two eyes, each of which receives a slightly different image of the object being looked at. The discrepancy between these two images furnishes very important cues about the relative depth of surfaces in a scene, known as **stereoscopic depth cues**. In contrast, Marr's program, for reasons of simplicity, deals with images as discrete, static entities; there is one light-sensitive screen in the computer, rather than the two retinae whose images can be compared.

In conclusion, the 'successes' of Marr's model indicate that quite complex objects can be correctly segregated by the bottom-up application of general Gestalt grouping principles. The fact that a number of objects have been correctly segregated in this way suggests that Marr's model does provide an analogy for the grouping operations of a natural vision system.

On the other hand, Marr's model 'fails' at assemblies of objects which pose no problem for us visually. This failure is uninformative about whether such ambiguities are resolved bottom-up or top-down in a natural vision system, although the indications are that enough cues are often available to the natural vision system for bottom-up resolution. The one useful insight which comes from this failure of Marr's vision system is an idea of the additional operations which must be added to the system if it is to utilize all the cues available to a natural vision system. If you wish to read more about computational attempts to solve the problems of seeing in depth, you should consult Bruce and Green (1990).

Summary of Section 4

- The Gestalt laws specify the conditions under which elements of patterns will be perceptually grouped into coherent structures having emergent properties not found in the original elements.
- Gestalt laws of proximity, similarity, good continuity and closure are all instances of a more basic Law of Prägnanz, according to which the perceptual organization which actually occurs will be the one which possesses the best, simplest and most stable shape.
- Experimental work has provided objective correlates for these phenomena. This suggests a role for Gestalt grouping processes in 'assembling' those components of input which are likely to belong together as parts of the same object.
- Marr's full primal sketch stage relies on Gestalt grouping principles to make explicit the contour of a single object. The outline of the principle internal structures can be asserted in the same way.
- Implementations of Marr's model have in some cases been successful in resolving ambiguities about which primitives from the raw

primal sketch 'go together'. However, with objects such as overlapping leaves, the computer can only resolve the ambiguities by access to top-down knowledge.

- Natural visual systems have access to additional cues which may enable them to resolve such ambiguities by bottom-up processing.

5   *Object recognition: general requirements*

The discussion in the last section focused upon the processes which interpret input to the visual system as coherent structures, segregated from one another and from their background. This is, however, a long way from explaining how the objects which provide the source for these structures are recognized.

Object recognition has proved the most difficult stage for theories of vision to explain in any detail. Many of the 'models' which have been proposed, including Marr's, simply address one or more of the general requirements for recognition (thus stating a computational theory) rather than specifying the algorithms or processes which will implement these requirements. This section will look at these general requirements. The next section will consider a single more comprehensive model.

The main points can be illustrated by reference to a four-legged mammal like the donkey shown in Figure 2.18. Early visual processing

Figure 2.18   How do we recognize natural objects such as donkeys?

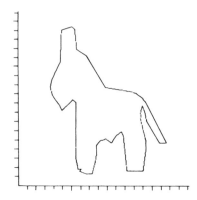

Figure 2.19   Full primal sketch outline derived from the image of a toy donkey   (Marr and Nishihara, 1978, Figure 6a)

stages like those described in Sections 3 and 4 would yield a description of the overall shape of the object. Figure 2.19 shows such an outline, derived in this case from the image of a toy donkey.

How is this 2-D outline processed further to provide a basis for recognizing a 3-D object? Some models propose a subsequent 2.5D sketch, which delivers precise and accurate information about the layout of object surfaces in space — their distance from each other and from the viewer. This constitutes an overall representation of the three-dimensional characteristics of scenes containing one or more objects. We need this kind of information in order to move around the environment, touching things, and picking them up without bumping into them. However, there is evidence that this stage in visual processing may not be an interim stage contributing directly to object recognition. Thus, this discussion will simply note the importance of this stage for human action on the environment. (For further discussion of the cues which enable both humans and computers to 'see' and respond to 3-D scenes, consult Bruce and Green, 1990.)

The crucial point for object recognition is that input which has been processed to the stage of a primal sketch, and perhaps beyond, must now be processed to yield a description which provides the basis for identification. This description needs to be in an appropriate form to be compared with visually-based descriptions of object categories stored in memory (e.g. it needs to match a stored description of what a donkey looks like). Four main problems must be addressed:

1 What primitives are used in the description (i.e. what basic elements or parts are used to describe objects as a basis for recognition)?
2 How is the relationship between these elements specified?
3 How is the overall description specified in a form which is invariant across viewpoints?

4 What representation and what matching process results in the categorization of visually different objects as belonging to the same
category?

These problems are considered in turn in Section 5.

5.1   Primitives

Besides our intuitive sense that the parts of an object such as a dog are
relevant to its description, there is experimental evidence like that
from Part I. From Rosch's studies we saw that subjects spontaneously
treat parts such as 'legs', 'ears', 'tail' as features which characterize
object categories. But considered as a basis for describing the visual
appearance of different objects, these intuitive parts may pose a problem: the 'legs' of one animal, say a dog, may appear visually very
different from the 'legs' of another such as bird. Most researchers have
therefore sought to express these intuitive features in terms of a relatively small set of basic primitives which will be invariant components
of a variety of different objects.

Marr working with Nishihara (1978) proposed that a system of **generalized cylinders** at different levels of resolution would do the job.
The application of this system to the representation of a horse is shown
in Figure 2.20.

As is clear, cylinders provide a plausible set of components for this
particular case, and the assumption is that the same set of components
will serve in different combinations and sizes for other objects, as shown
in Figure 2.21.

Figure 2.20   Generalized cylinders used to represent a horse   (Marr and
Nishihara, 1978, Figure 8)

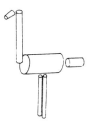

Figure 2.21   An ostrich can be represented using the same system of generalized cylinders   (Marr and Nishihara, 1978, Figure 8)

The decision as to exactly how an object is divided up into components, each represented by a cylinder, is not arbitrary. Marr and Nishihara showed that the 'right' decisions are made if the primal sketch object outline is divided up at regions of deep **concavity** (i.e. where one part of the object outline makes a sharp angle with another). Figure 2.22 shows a primal sketch outline of the toy donkey shown in Figure 2.19 with convex and concave sections labelled with '+' and '−' respectively.

These concave and convex sections are then used as a basis for dividing the outline into smaller regions, a process known as **parsing** or **segmentation**. Each of these regions is then represented by a cylinder at an appropriate level of resolution.

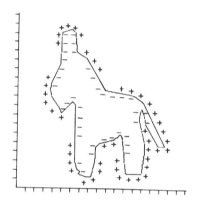

Figure 2.22   Full primal sketch outline derived from image of toy donkey, with convex (+) and concave (−) sections marked   (Marr and Nishihara, 1978, Figure 6b)

Marr and Nishihara's primitives were designed to be suitable for a wide range of objects. 'Generalized' cylinder means that the basic shape component does not need to have a straight axis — this provides for cases such as a G-shaped or S-shaped tube. Similarly, the diameter of the 'cylinder' need not be uniform: objects such as an hour-glass or a bell can be accommodated by building a varying diameter parameter into the description. But there are many objects (chairs, houses, crumpled sheets of paper) for which the generalized cylinder would provide an inadequate descriptive component. Since this stage of Marr's model still assumes no prior (top-down) knowledge about the identity of objects to which the components are applied, the implication is that the system would make incorrect assertions for these sorts of objects. Biederman's model, which we shall look at in Section 6, seeks to improve on Marr's proposal about primitives.

5.2   Relations between primitives: structural descriptions

Not only the basic components but also the way they fit together must be specified if they are to provide a basis for recognizing objects and distinguishing them from one another. So-called **structural descriptions** provide a general framework for object recognition, based on this proposal.

Formally speaking, a structural description is a set of propositions about a pattern from which the actual pattern may be generated. It consists of the parts of the pattern together with the rules for linking them up. Exactly the same definition applies to objects, which can be thought of as complex three-dimensional patterns.

SAQ 16
Consider the letters 'b', 'd' and 'p'. A simple list of their features (straight line and closed loop) is the same for all three letters. This alone could not provide a basis for distinguishing between them.

Imagine that you are describing these letters to a friend who has to identify them from your description, or write them on paper. What is the minimum information which your friend needs about each letter?

The answer to SAQ 16 consists of simple structural descriptions. They represent the letters in terms of features, together with rules defining the structural relationships between the features. Of course, the structural descriptions in the SAQ answer are for 2-D patterns (letters). In the present case, we are interested in a system of structural descriptions which could provide the basis for characterizing 3-D objects. How can the relationships among the components be specified in a way which captures the characteristic shapes of these objects?

As we have seen, Marr and Nishihara's proposals are built on the notion of the generalized cylinder as the basic primitive. Structural relations are expressed by a hierarchical organization of these primitives, in which the overall shape of the object is represented by a generalized cylinder at the coarsest level of resolution, and this is gradually decomposed or broken down into component cylinders in which the detail is revealed (see Figure 2.23 overleaf). Each cylinder is treated as having its own axis, and the way in which the various cylinder axes are joined to one another is expressed in a coordinate system (similar to plotting the position of all the components on a three-dimensional graph).

Again, this is just one example of the way in which structural relationships can be expressed.

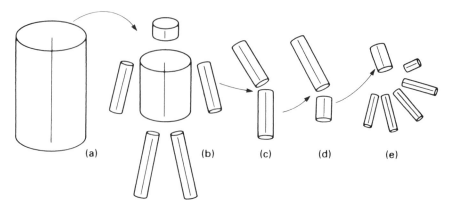

Figure 2.23   Hierarchical organization of generalized cylinders representing a human figure: (a) coarsest level — overall cylinder with axis indicating main orientation of figure; (b) cylinders representing parts at next level of resolution — axes indicate structural relationships between parts; (c) upper and lower arm cylinders derived from overall arm cylinder in (b); (d) cylinders representing lower arm components consisting of forearm and hand; (e) cylinders representing hand components consisting of palm and fingers   (based on Marr and Nishihara, 1978, Figure 3)

5.3   Invariance across viewpoints: object-centred structural descriptions

It has already been stressed that if an object description is to provide a basis for recognition it needs to apply regardless of the viewpoint from which it is seen: otherwise, the continued existence of an object will not be recognized when the viewer or the object moves. The problem is well illustrated by the line drawings in Figures 2.3a and 2.3b in Section 1 (see page 75).

Each of the following structural descriptions could be used to describe the line drawing in Figure 2.3a:

(i)   Nine straight lines, joined in a particular way, and including three short horizontals and three short verticals all of the same length, and three long diagonals, all of the same length. (N.B. A proper structural description would specify the rules linking the lines, but they are omitted for brevity.)

(ii)   Three regions, a square and two parallelograms, joined together in a particular way.

(iii)   Two-dimensional representation of a three-dimensional cuboid, having two square surfaces and four rectangular surfaces, of particular sizes.

Only one of the three descriptions also applies to Figure 2.3b, which we recognize as the same object viewed from a different angle.

SAQ 17
Which of the three descriptions applies to both line drawings? Why is it only this description which applies to both line drawings?

This example makes the point that structural descriptions must be object-centred, but it does not indicate what characteristics of input can be used to derive such object-centred descriptions. Palmer (1992) proposed the intrinsic **frame of reference** of objects as a basis. This is illustrated in the following example.

Figure 2.24a depicts the same schematic human face at four different orientations. If we were merely to describe the pattern of features in each of the examples, relative to our own orientation to the object, it would be different in each case. (For instance, the description 'two oval blobs at the top, triangular blob in the middle, curved line at the bottom' would only apply to the face on the top left.)

A single, orientation-invariant way of describing the four faces becomes possible if the intrinsic axes of the schematic face are drawn in, as in Figure 2.24b.

A-B is the axis of symmetry of the face (i.e. the line which divides the face into two identical halves); C-D is the central axis of the shape. It should be clear that a description of the internal structure of the face *relative to these axes* will be the same (i.e. invariant) regardless of the orientation of the face relative to the external world (and to the retina). For a completely invariant description, the same principle must be applied to each of the components of the face, and the part descriptions related to the overall reference frame. This is shown for the eye feature in Figure 2.24c.

The principle of reference frames is used to provide object-centred descriptions in Marr and Nishihara's proposals for object recognition. Each of the generalized cylinders which serves as an object component has its own intrinsic frame of reference: in this case, the central axis of

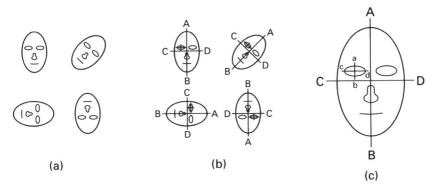

(a)   (b)   (c)

Figure 2.24   Intrinsic axes used to provide a frame of reference   (adapted from Palmer, 1992)

the cylinder. The position of each cylinder is described relative to its own axis, resulting in a description which is invariant across viewpoints. The structural relationship of all the cylinders is in turn expressed in terms of the relations between the axes, resulting in an overall description which is invariant across views.

5.4   Descriptions for matching with visual object categories

So far in this section, we have considered the requirements for describing or representing a single object so that it is identifiable across a variety of viewpoints. However, when we recognize objects we also assign visually different objects to a single category: chairs, for instance, come in a variety of shapes and sizes.

Part I addressed the general nature of the representations responsible for categorizing objects, but did not deal with the special case of categorization (recognition) from visual characteristics alone, which is the focus of Part II. An attempt will be made here to put together the ideas discussed in the two parts.

Part I suggested that the representation of an object category might consist of one or more of the following types of representation:

1 A list of defining features (both perceptual and non-perceptual) constituting a definition applicable to all category members.
2 A list of features (both perceptual and non-perceptual) which characterize the most typical category members.
3 Multiple representations (each comprising both perceptual and non-perceptual characteristics) corresponding to specific exemplars.

We have seen that the features or components adequate for recognizing objects from their visual characteristics alone probably need to consist of shape primitives which have a common description across a variety of different objects. The *relationship* between these primitives, in the form of structural descriptions, also becomes important in providing a basis for visual recognition. How then might these structural descriptions map on to the three types of representations of object categories listed above?

1 *Structural descriptions as category definitions*
In principle, a structural description could serve as a definition of an object category which applied equally to all category members. This assumption was implicitly adopted by Marr and Nishihara. Animal categories, such as 'giraffe', 'horse', 'elephant', 'human', were each assumed to be represented by a single structural description depicting a definitional arrangement of cylindrical components within a three-dimensional coordinate system.

It is notable that Marr and Nishihara developed their general scheme with *animals* in mind: some animal categories may lend themselves to a definitional-type visual shape description. But this proposal would probably run into difficulties with animals such as dogs, where different breeds have highly distinctive visual appearances. A single definition would be unlikely to cover such variety.

2   *Structural descriptions as typical feature summaries*
Categories of artefacts such as 'chair', 'table', etc. would almost certainly pose problems for structural descriptions considered as definitions. It is particularly in terms of visual characteristics that these categories comprise a diversity of examples. Even if these categories have dual representations, as suggested by Armstrong et al., the representation used for rapid perceptual identification is likely to be the 'everyday' (fuzzy) representation.

A summary structural description suitable for visually recognizing members of categories such as 'chair' would need to be tolerant of a degree of diversity among category exemplars. It is not entirely clear how this tolerance would be built in. Chairs, for instance, display a variety of angles between seat and backrest, so it might be necessary to specify an 'acceptable' range of angles in the structural description of typical chairs.

It is, however, no coincidence that much of object recognition occurs at the basic level. Members of basic level categories are *relatively* similar to one another in appearance, and the representations for these categories are *relatively* well defined. Structural descriptions which typify basic level categories seem plausible, whereas structural descriptions for superordinate categories such as 'furniture' do not.

3   *Structural descriptions as multiple exemplar representations*
Structural descriptions could also be realized as multiple exemplar representations. In this case, the perceptual representation of a basic level object category would consist of separate structural descriptions for a number of different stored category exemplars. Each of these structural descriptions could be quite finely adjusted to the characteristics of the exemplar it represented. Consequently, it would not matter if the category exemplars so represented were quite unlike one another. It follows that structural descriptions, deployed in this fashion, would be well suited to represent categories with diverse members, such as dogs. However, as we saw in Part I, there is still the problem of which exemplars from the total set are represented.

Besides specifying the nature of visual category representations, models of object recognition need to make explicit the matching process by which inputs in the form of structural descriptions are matched with stored representations. An important question is whether the decision to assign an input to a given category is made solely on the basis of such a match, or is influenced by top-down information about the interpretation that is most likely given the context.

Up to now, the stages resulting in object recognition have been described in bottom-up terms. The underlying assumption has been that a series of bottom-up stages will serve to resolve ambiguities about the significance of input sufficiently to permit correct identification of objects: earlier stages have served to resolve ambiguities about 'what goes with what'; later stages have sought to specify both the components of objects and their relationship in a form which is unambiguous across viewpoints. However, at each stage ambiguities arose. It was not clear whether these ambiguities could be resolved bottom-up, or would require an additional input of top-down information.

Further opportunities for ambiguity arise at the matching-for-identification stage. In particular, information about the shape of the object may be missing, as when an object in a scene is partially obscured by another object. Structural descriptions need to be 'robust' enough to tolerate such deficiencies. This problem is directly addressed, broadly in bottom-up terms, by Biederman's model, to be considered next.

Other sources of ambiguity arise when the object in question is an atypical category member. As we saw, a single structural description may be 'intolerant' of an object which has visual features quite different from the typical ones. Even multiple structural descriptions (as in exemplar models) are unlikely to accommodate atypical cases. In these cases, we need to consider whether top-down knowledge may be required to infer what an object is likely to be in a given context (see Labov's experiment in Part I, Techniques Box D).

Summary of Section 5

- Models for object recognition need to specify:

  A set of basic primitives which will serve to describe a variety of different objects;

  How these primitives are related;

  How the resulting structural description is rendered invariant across viewpoints;

  How this description is matched to stored representations to provide correct object categorization.

- Marr and Nishihara proposed that primitives consist of generalized cylinders with structural relations specified in a coordinate system.

- Palmer has provided evidence that an object's intrinsic frame of reference offers a basis for object-centred structural descriptions.
- Structural descriptions need to serve as visual representations for basic level object categories. There may be one such structural description per category (defining feature and typical feature models) or several (exemplar models).
- The structural description(s) needs to be tolerant of a range of characteristics among category members.
- Ambiguities may arise in object identification if information is missing and/or if the structural description is not adequate for all category members.

6 Object recognition: Biederman's model

Biederman's model (Biederman, 1987) has been primarily formulated as a model of *human* object recognition in contrast to Marr's model which is heavily influenced by AI.

Biederman's model takes as its starting point the everyday observation that if we are asked to give a description of an object, whether familiar or unfamiliar, we tend to employ the same basic strategy.

SAQ 18
Try to write down a description of the object in Figure 2.25.

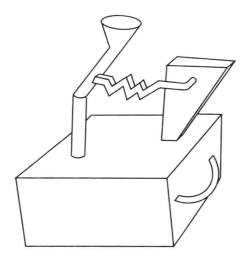

Figure 2.25 A 'do-it-yourself' object   (adapted from Biederman, 1987, Figure 1)

In order to describe the object, you almost certainly divided it into parts or components. This constitutes a process of parsing or segmentation, comparable to the parsing assumed by Marr and Nishihara. Moreover, as in Marr and Nishihara's proposals, the regions of the object which you used to divide it up were probably the regions of deep concavity (i.e. where one part makes a sharp angle with another part of the object). However, the list of components you employed almost certainly consisted of a variety of three-dimensional shape concepts (such as a 'block', a 'cylinder', a 'funnel', or a 'wedge'), not merely cylinders as suggested by Marr and Nishihara. Biederman refers to these as **volumetric concepts**.

Biederman claimed that this manner of segmenting objects is more than coincidental, and that it 'reflects the workings of the representational system by which objects are identified' (Biederman, 1987). For this reason, the model is known as **recognition-by-components**.

6.1   Primitives and structural relationships

The central claim of recognition-by-components, is that the primitives for object recognition consist of a reasonably small set (approximately 36) of simple volumetric shapes such as cylinders, blocks, wedges, and cones. These are known as **geons**. Geons from this same basic set, put together in a variety of different ways, can yield structural descriptions for a very large range of different objects.

Figure 2.26 shows some of the everyday objects which can be derived when the same geons are put together in different ways.

Figure 2.26 Different arrangements of the same geon components can produce different objects   (Biederman, 1987, Figure 3)

SAQ 19
(a) Make a list of the geon components which provide the basic elements of the four objects (use sketches if you prefer).
(b) How is the role of structural descriptions in object recognition illustrated by these examples?

Biederman suggests that just a small number of structural relationships provide the basis for generating a very large number of objects. The most obvious of these relationships are listed below for the hypothetical case of just two geons, G1 and G2. These could be, for instance, the rectangular block geon and the curved arc geon shown in Figure 2.26.

Relative size
For any pair of geons G1 and G2, G1 could be much greater than, smaller than, or approximately equal to G2.

Verticality
G1 can be above, below or to the side of G2.

Centring
The end to side join of G1 to G2 can be centred or non-centred (a special case is where two components are actually joined end-to-end, as in the upper and lower parts of the human arm).

Relative size of surfaces at join
Almost all geons (except spheres and cubes) have a long and a short surface. The join between geons G1 and G2 can be on either surface.

The following description applies to the 'attaché case' in Figure 2.26, with values of the four structural relationships specified (G1 = rectangular block; G2 = curved arc):
    Relative size: G1 bigger than G2
    Verticality: G1 below G2
    Centring: G2 centred on G1 at join
    Relative size of surfaces at join: G2 joined to a long surface of G1

SAQ 20
Now write out a similar structural description for the 'slide drawer' shown in Figure 2.26.

6.2   *Invariance across viewpoints*

The basis for invariance in Biederman's model again marks a contrast with Marr and Nishihara's proposals.

In Biederman's model, the geons are described in terms of simple characteristics which occur in the edges derived from two-dimensional images (the full primal sketch in Marr's model). These edges are said to have characteristics which are related in a *non-accidental* way to the edges of objects in the real world. A similar idea was discussed in Section 4.2, where we saw that Gestalt groupings of elements are non-accidental in the sense that they correspond to significant properties of objects.

In recognition-by-components, non-accidental properties are characteristics such as a straight edge: this is likely to correspond to a straight edge in the object from which it derives. Similarly, a curved edge is likely to correspond to a curved edge in the object from which it derives. Only in rare accidental cases, when the eye views an object from a very unusual angle, does a straight edge in an image derive from a curved edge in the object.

Table 2.2   Biederman's five non-accidental properties and their associated 3-D assertions

2-D property	3-D assertion
Collinearity: Points or line segments in a line	Parts of object lie along a straight line in 3-D space
Curvilinearity: Points or arc segments form a curve	Parts of object lie along a curve in 3-D space
Symmetry: 2-D outline is made up of symmetrical elements	Parts of object are symmetrical in 3-D space
Parallel curves: 2-D outline contains parallel curves	Parts of object form parallel curves in 3-D space
Co-termination: Two or more lines end at a common point	Edges of object terminate at a common point in 3-D space

Biederman argues that non-accidental properties such as straight or curved edges are themselves invariant: their correspondence with object properties remains the same regardless of the location from which the object is viewed. What this means is that invariant, three-dimensional properties of objects can be inferred directly from two-dimensional properties of the full primal sketch. Altogether, five non-accidental properties can be used in this way. These are listed in Table 2.2, together with the three-dimensional assertions which can be derived from them.

Biederman proposes that each of the geons (cylinders, blocks, wedges, etc.) in the basic set is assembled from a different set of values of these five non-accidental properties.

To summarize, Biederman's account of invariance assumes that simple two-dimensional properties of the primal sketch serve as invariants, from which object-centred descriptions of object components can be directly recovered. Not only the geons, but the structural descriptions which represent how the geons are related are assumed to be robust across viewpoints.

In contrast, Marr and Nishihara's model assumes that invariance is a function of the overall shape description which results when the appropriate arrangement of cylindrical components is recovered from the full primal sketch.

6.3 The process of object categorization

Biederman's assumptions about how a given object is assigned to the appropriate category are not worked out in detail. The main assumption is that the stored representations against which incoming object descriptions are to be compared consist of a 'catalogue' of the 36 geons in the basic set. The geons extracted from a given object are matched in parallel against these stored representations. However, besides the store of individual geons, there must presumably be a store of complete object descriptions in which both the characteristic geon set, and the relationships among them, are specified — otherwise complete objects could not be recognized. Finally, Biederman's account appears to assume that each basic level object category is represented by just one structural description which encapsulates either a definition or a summary of what is most visually typical of the category. However, Biederman gives little detail on this point.

We shall now look at some experimental tests of Biederman's model.

6.4 Experimental tests of Biederman's model

Biederman's model was designed: (1) to provide an intuitively plausible account of how we recognize objects in terms of their obvious components; and (2) to explain the fact that this recognition is both rapid and accurate, despite variations in the angle from which objects are viewed and the 'degraded' information which is available when lighting is poor, or one object obscures another.

One general prediction from the model is that, since an appropriate arrangement of geons provides a very powerful cue for object recognition, this recognition will occur even when an object's full complement of geons are not present. A test of this prediction is described in Techniques Box K.

TECHNIQUES BOX K

Speed and Accuracy in Perceiving Incomplete Objects
(Biederman, 1987)

Rationale

1 To investigate speed and accuracy in identifying objects presented with some geon components missing.
2 To investigate the effects of complexity (defined in terms of number of geons) on object identification.

Method

Line drawings of 36 common objects were prepared. These differed in their 'complexity', defined in terms of how many basic geon components were needed to draw them. Levels of complexity were: 2, 3, 4, 6 and 9 components. For each line drawing, 'partial' versions were prepared in which one or more of the geon components were missing. Examples of complete and partial objects are shown in Figure 2.27. Each stimulus was presented for 100 milliseconds via a projection tachistoscope. The subject responded as fast as possible by naming the object aloud into a voice microphone. This is a device which deactivates a reaction timer activated by the onset of the display. Errors in naming were also recorded.

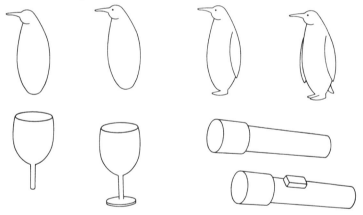

Figure 2.27 Complete and partial versions of objects used in Biederman's experiment: wine glass and torch are three-component objects; penguin is a nine-component object   (Biederman 1987, Figure 12)

Results

Error rates for 'partial' objects were extremely low. As shown in Figure 2.28, 90 per cent accuracy was achieved even for complex objects with two-thirds of their components missing. Reaction times were almost as rapid for partial objects as for complete objects. However, complex complete objects (those made up of many geons) were identified slightly faster than simple ones.

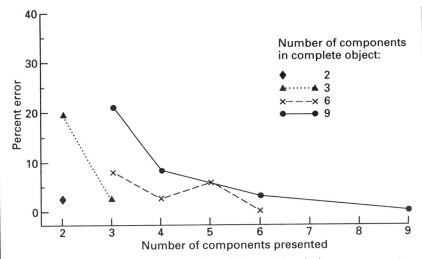

Figure 2.28   Error rates for naming objects with missing components. The percentage of errors (vertical axis) is plotted against the number of components in the presented objects (horizontal axis). Separate functions are shown for two-, three-, six- and nine-component objects (Biederman, 1987, Figure 14)

The results are generally in keeping with the recognition-by-components model in showing that even the simplest partial line drawings of objects can be rapidly and correctly identified provided relevant geons are present. The slight advantage for identifying objects composed of many geons is also in keeping with the model's assumption that an object's geons are simultaneously matched with stored geon descriptions. The more of such geons that are available, the more quickly will the criterion level necessary for a 'match' be reached.

A more stringent test of the model relies on testing subjects' ability to identify degraded versions of objects (i.e. those in which the normal contours of objects are disrupted). According to the model, forms of degradation which disrupt the basis for identifying geons should have a profound impact on the ability to recognize objects, whereas degradation which leaves this information intact should not. For examples of 'recognizable' and 'non-recognizable' objects, see Figure 2.29 overleaf.

In the middle column of Figure 2.29, the contours of objects have been deleted in regions where they can be replaced by applying the principles of collinearity and curvilinearity. The objects are recognizable. In the right-hand column, contours have been deleted at regions of concavity (i.e. at sharp angles which are important for dividing the objects into geons). Application of the principles of collinearity and curvilinearity would 'bridge' these angles rather than reinstating them. The components of the objects cannot be made out, hence the objects are non-recognizable.

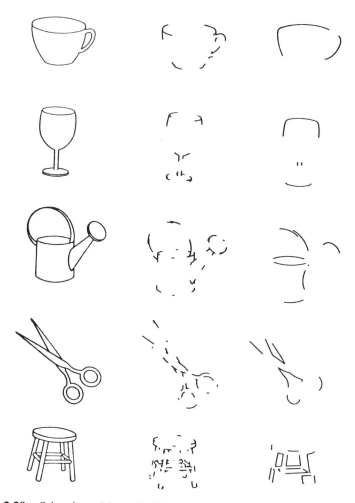

Figure 2.29 Stimulus objects in Biederman's experiment with two types of degradation. The left-hand column shows complete objects; the middle column shows 'recognizable' versions; and the right-hand column shows the 'non-recognizable' versions   (Biederman, 1987, Figure 16)

The experimental procedure was similar to that in Techniques Box K. Stimuli were presented for 100, 200 or 750 milliseconds, and with 25 per cent, 45 per cent or 65 per cent of contours removed. In keeping with the model, the results showed that subjects were markedly slow and inaccurate at identifying the non-recognizable object versions, whereas the effects for the 'recognizable' versions were slight. It seems that disruption of the non-accidental properties from which geons are constructed does have a marked effect on recognition.

6.5   *Evaluation of recognition-by-components*

Biederman's model addresses several of the requirements for object recognition more satisfactorily than earlier proposals, such as those of Marr and Nishihara.

The geon primitives in Biederman's model not only accord well with our intuitions, but appear to offer a relatively flexible and comprehensive system for describing objects. Marr and Nishihara's generalized cylinder, though well suited to representing the parts of mammals and other animals, is unsuited to describing artifacts such as chairs, tables, houses, etc. Biederman's geons include a range of different shapes to cover these possibilities. Biederman's structural description system again accords well with intuitions, and requires only a limited range of values of each relationship. Marr and Nishihara's concept of a 3-D coordinate system with an infinite range of values may be well-suited for vision machines which, with their infinite capacity can compute the coordinates of each new object afresh, but might require long processing times in a human visual system.

The source for invariance in Biederman's model (the non-accidental properties present in the primal sketch) makes elegant use of Gestalt-type processes to generate not only orientation-invariant geons but also orientation-invariant geon relations. In Marr and Nishihara's account, orientation-invariance emerges as a property of the three-dimensional object description.

Finally, Biederman's model has generated empirical hypotheses which have been tested. The results are consistent with the model, and, in particular, suggest that geon descriptions may be robust in conditions where stimulus input is degraded or partial, an important feature of natural vision. In contrast, Marr and Nishihara's ideas consist of general proposals. The fact that these have been difficult to implement casts doubts on their viability.

Biederman's model also has drawbacks. In particular, the identification of the 36 geons and their structural relations is based more on intuition than empirical test: it is not yet clear whether this basic set of 36 geons provides a comprehensive basis for characterizing object categories. Nor is there any direct proof that the particular non-accidental properties listed by Biederman are actually those used in object recognition. Experiment results are consistent with the model, but do not provide critical tests of it.

Finally, Biederman's model represents little advance on Marr and Nishihara's model in explaining the nature of the representation for complete basic level object categories, and the way inputs are matched to these. The organization of this stage remains unclear. The next section considers this visual recognition process from a different angle: the fact that once we have recognized an object from its appearance, we also know what it is for and what it is called.

Summary of Section 6

- Biederman's recognition-by-components model assumes that the basic primitives for recognizing objects consist of geons: volumetric concepts such as blocks, cylinders, cones, and wedges.
- A set of 36 geons, together with a small set of structural relations such as relative size and position, are sufficient to generate a wide variety of different objects.
- The source of invariance in recognition-by-components is found in non-accidental properties of the primal sketch, such as collinearity and symmetry.
- Biederman's model offers advantages over earlier approaches in terms of intuitive plausibility, parsimony and empirical support.
- However, the major assumptions of the model have not been critically tested, and the model is unspecific about the processes and representations responsible for correct basic level categorization.

7 Beyond recognition: using and naming

Up to now, we have been concerned with the representations and processes which enable a person (or an artificial vision system) to recognize a visually presented object. We have devoted little discussion to what information is made available when recognition occurs. In Biederman's experiments, subjects were assumed to have recognized an object if they were able to name it correctly, but in practice there are three distinct though interrelated aspects to recognition:

1 *Familiarity*
The person reports that an object 'looks' familiar. This implies that the visual characteristics of the object match stored structural knowledge of previously encountered objects.

2 *Function/use*
The person can give a correct account of what the object does or what it is used for (e.g. a person who sees a cow describes it as an animal which is kept by farmers, eats grass and provides milk). In this case, the visual characteristics of the object have enabled the person to access **semantic knowledge** about the animal.

3 *Name*
The person can name the object correctly. In this case the object's visual characteristics and/or semantic characteristics have enabled the person to access its **name**.

Intuitively at least, we can thus distinguish three aspects of recognition, and this section will consider the relationship between them. Are they all combined within a single processing module or do they constitute separate stages? If the stages are separate, are they completely independent of each other? These three hypothetical stages will be referred to as structural description, semantic, and name respectively.

7.1   Separate stages?

Rosch's typical feature model, discussed in Part I, assumed that a category such as 'chair' was represented by a single list of typical features, including both perceptual information (legs, backrest) and non-perceptual information (used for sitting on). By implication, the category name also constituted part of the representation. In Rosch's model then, structural, semantic, and name information are assumed to be stored together.

However, Rosch's model was not formulated to bear directly on *visual* object recognition, and it does seem clear that people have the ability to recognize objects on the basis of visual characteristics alone. This argues for an initial visual recognition stage (a structural description stage), with semantic recognition (e.g. recognizing what an object is for) and naming (giving the object its appropriate name) as subsequent stages. The assumption of a separate structural stage is implicit in both Marr and Nishihara's and Biederman's models.

The most compelling evidence for a separation of structural, semantic and naming stages comes from neuropsychological studies by researchers such as Humphreys (see, for instance, Humphreys and Bruce, 1989). These studies focus on individuals who, as a result of brain lesions, are unable to recognize visually presented objects. The crucial question is whether this kind of deficit represents a global loss of structural, semantic and naming aspects of recognition, or whether one or more of these abilities remain intact. The former finding would imply an integration of structural, semantic and naming stages, while the latter would imply separate stages.

Careful investigation of recognition abilities in a range of patients reveals a pattern of findings consistent with the separate stage hypothesis. Depending on the nature and extent of their brain damage, different individuals display selective loss of some aspects of recognition while others remain intact. More specifically, these patients differ along two dimensions relevant to the separate stage hypothesis, namely:

1 which aspects of recognition (structural, semantic, naming) are lost;
2 whether their deficits arise from loss of the relevant stored representations from memory or from inability to *access* these representations.

To spell out these points, let's consider two patients, referred to as JB and HJA, who have been extensively studied by Humphreys et al. (1988) and Humphreys and Riddoch (1987). Neuropsychological assessments and experiments were employed in detailed single case studies of these two patients, both of whom displayed marked deficits in the ability to name pictorially presented objects.

JB developed this deficit following brain damage sustained in a road accident. Although unable to name pictured objects, he could recognize the same objects by touch, and he was also able to give correct names when provided with a verbal definition. JB was also able to make appropriate semantic associations between objects. For instance, if given the names 'hammer', 'nail' and 'screw', he was able to say which two of the three went together. He was unable to perform the same task if shown the same objects visually.

HJA developed the inability to name pictorially presented objects after bilateral brain damage following a stroke. However, HJA retained the ability to copy line drawings of objects and to draw objects from memory if given their names.

Both these case outlines suggest that the patients retained some skills relevant to recognition, and this supports the hypothesis of separate recognition stages. Humphreys and his co-workers sought to investigate these components further with experiments designed to pinpoint the source of the patients' naming deficits. An experiment designed to investigate loss of structural recognition is reported in Techniques Box L.

TECHNIQUES BOX L

Neuropsychological Studies of Object Recognition Failure
(Humphreys et al., 1988; Humphreys and Riddoch, 1987)

Rationale
To investigate, in the cases of JB and HJA:
1 Whether they retained intact representations of how objects should look (i.e. intact structural knowledge).
2 Whether they could access this knowledge when presented with pictures of objects.

Method
Both subjects were asked to sort pictures of objects into piles according to whether they were 'real' (meaningful) or 'unreal' (meaningless). The real objects came from familiar superordinate categories (animals, household objects, etc.). The meaningless objects were constructed by replacing a feature of each object with one from another object. These substituted features either came from another object within the same superordinate category (e.g. a sheep would be shown with its head replaced by the head of a dog), or from another superordinate category (e.g. a donkey might be shown with its tail

---

replaced by a door handle). Because the task requires sorting rather than naming, it tests the patients' visual recognition abilities independently of their ability to name the objects.

Results
JB's performance on the task was as good as that of controls, whereas HJA's performance was very poor compared with controls.

Conclusions
1 The fact that one subject (JB) was able to carry out the visual recognition task, despite being unable to name the objects, provides strong evidence in support of a separate structural stage.
2 JB's performance indicates that he both knew what objects should look like (i.e. his store of structural representations was intact) and could access this knowledge. This implies that JB's naming problem lay beyond the structural stage. Yet, as described in his case history, JB appeared to have intact semantic knowledge of objects, since he was able to make correct semantic associations between object words such as 'hammer' and 'nail'. Putting these findings together, it appears that JB's problem lay *after* the structural recognition stage, but before a hypothetical semantic recognition stage. By implication, JB had a problem in *accessing* semantic information about objects, after recognizing them by their appearance.
3 HJA's performance shows that he was unable to employ structural knowledge in order to distinguish real objects from unreal objects. Yet, as described in his case history, HJA knew how objects should look, since he could draw them from memory. It follows that HJA's problem was one of *accessing* structural knowledge when presented with visual objects.

SAQ 21
One aspect of JB's performance poses a puzzle for Humphrey's account of his deficit: he was able to make appropriate gestures to objects he could not name (e.g. a digging movement in response to a spade). What difficulty does this imply for Humphrey's account?

Similar methods to those just described were used to provide evidence for the separate semantic recognition stage implied by JB's case history. Results from a number of patients are generally in keeping with the idea that structural, semantic and name stages follow one another. The claim that naming comes last in this sequence is well supported by the clinical data: there appear to be no cases in which patients retain the ability to name objects having lost the ability to recognize them by visual and/or semantic characteristics.

The data thus support the idea of separable structural, semantic and name stages arranged in sequence, but this does not necessarily mean that these stages are independent of one another. We shall now look at two different conceptualizations of these stages.

7.2 Models of the relationship between structural, semantic and name stages

The most obvious model reflecting a separation of structural, semantic and name stages is a bottom-up sequence of stages, in which one stage of processing is completed before the subsequent stage begins (see Figure 2.30).

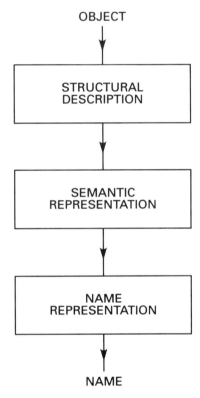

Figure 2.30 A discrete stage model of structural, semantic and name stages (based on Humphreys et al., 1988, Figure 1)

According to this model, the first stage of recognition consists of matching the structural characteristics of the object to a stored structural description. Once a match has been achieved, the result is signalled to the semantic representation stage so that semantic characteristics of the object can be accessed. Again, once this process is completed, the result is signalled to the name stage so that a name for the object is accessed.

Humphreys et al. (1988) propose an alternative model in which separable structural, semantic and name stages interact with one another, as shown in Figure 2.31.

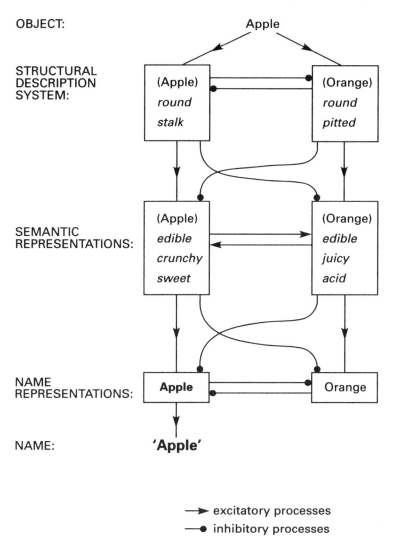

Figure 2.31   A cascade model of structural, semantic and name stages (based on Humphreys et al., 1988, Figure 2)

This model assumes that while the processing does proceed across an ordered sequence of stages, these stages are not independent: there is an interaction of information both within and between stages. The model is known as a **cascade model** to denote the continuous flow of information through the system.

Broadly speaking, when a person sees an object (or a picture of an object), such as an apple, information consistent with the stored structural description for an apple starts to 'activate' the appropriate structural description. But since apples are visually somewhat similar to other fruit such as oranges, information relevant to the structural description for orange also begins to accumulate. In order to prevent an inappropriate 'match' with the structural description for orange, the model postulates 'inhibitory' links between structural description nodes: the more information which accumulates in favour of apple, the more inhibition is exerted on the structural description stage. Information favouring the structural description 'apple' is also transmitted up to the next stage to begin activating the appropriate semantic representation. Some (but less) information relevant to the semantic representation for orange is also transmitted to the next stage. Since both apple and orange belong to the same semantic category, 'fruit', the model shows some mutual excitation between the semantic representations for apple and orange. However, any excitation for orange at this stage will be powerfully offset by inhibition coming from the structural description for apple. Further processes of excitation and inhibition occur at the next stage where information relevant to the name 'apple' is accumulating. A trickle of information relevant to the name 'orange' is transmitted but this is cancelled by the powerful inhibition coming from both semantic and name representations for apple. Over a period of time, this system will achieve a steady state in which the structural, semantic and name representations corresponding to the presented object (apple in this case) are activated up to some threshold point for recognition, while activity of other candidate representations (those for orange in this case) are inhibited and remain below threshold.

This model and the earlier independent stage model make different predictions about how subjects will perform in object-naming tasks. Specifically, the cascade model predicts that recognition difficulties at a particular source point (say the access route from structural to semantic stages) will have 'knock on' effects: they will be transmitted up the system from one stage to the next. In contrast, the independent stage model predicts that difficulties at a particular source point will not have 'knock-on' effects. These contrary predictions were tested in a further study of JB described in Techniques Box M.

TECHNIQUES BOX M

A Neuropsychological Study of Object Naming
(Humphreys et al., 1988)

Rationale
To investigate JB's performance in naming pictorially presented objects from categories with similar looking members vs categories with dissimilar members. The cascade model predicts that the similar looking category items will accentuate the difficulty in accessing relevant semantic information, which will in turn accentuate naming difficulty. The independent stage model predicts that the level of naming difficulty will be the same regardless of whether objects come from categories with 'similar' or 'dissimilar' members.

Method
JB was asked to name line drawings of objects drawn from twelve different categories. Six of these categories were judged as having members which look similar to one another: for instance, members of the category 'animal' or 'bird' tend to share many perceptual features in common. Six categories were judged to have structurally distinct exemplars: for instance, members of the category 'furniture' or 'clothes' tend to share few perceptual attributes in common.

Results
JB's ability to name the pictorially presented objects was markedly affected by the type of category they came from: for instance, he named only 17.6 per cent of animals correctly, whereas he named 88.9 per cent of clothes correctly.

Conclusions
Humphreys et al. interpreted these results as further evidence for a difficulty, in JB's case, in accessing semantic information from the structural stage. Any special 'load' on this access route, as when objects are visually similar to other objects, impairs access to semantic information about what they are, and what they are used for, and this in turn makes the objects difficult to name. The pattern of results is consistent with the cascade model. The model assumes that naming depends on semantic recognition which in turn depends on visual recognition. Using visually confusable objects appears to have had 'knock on' effects, making it more difficult to identify their category (semantic characteristics) and hence more difficult to name them.

To conclude, Humphrey's studies of patients like JB provide some powerful insights into the high level processes which contribute to object recognition. The evidence strongly suggests that this recognition consists of separable structural, semantic and naming components. However, studies like that in Techniques Box M also indicate that these processes overlap in time and interact with one another. The results obtained with JB were mirrored in further studies with normal subjects.

Summary of Section 7

- There is both anecdotal and empirical evidence for a separation of structural, semantic and naming processes in recognition.
- Evidence from neuropsychological patients strongly supports this separation.
- Humphreys et al. have proposed that processing across these stages operates in cascade, rather than as a discrete sequence of independent stages.
- Studies of both neuropsychological patients and normal subjects display 'knock-on' effects across recognition stages, as predicted by the cascade model.

8   Conclusion

Part II has attempted to address the remarkably complex set of achievements represented by our ability to recognize objects. The guiding theme throughout has been to try to understand how, from an impoverished and variable 2-D retinal image, we construct representations which enable us to recognize the appearance of objects, know what they are used for, and what they are called.

The strategy of going stage-by-stage from the retina, treating visual processes as a series of separable modules, arranged in sequence, is a heuristic device rather than necessarily a correct characterization of how objects are recognized: Marr's claim that visual processing works largely in a bottom-up direction does seem to work quite well as an account of the early visual processing stages: those leading up to the full primal sketch. But even at these early stages, this model is probably an oversimplification. Consideration of the way in which ambiguities are resolved at each stage in the processing of input has given evidence of some of the underlying complexities. Marr's system needed to rely upon a combination of general principles indicating the probable significance of input patterns, and, occasionally, upon hints coming from a top-down direction. It is not clear to what extent similar principles are employed in human visual processing, and to what extent the human visual system can 'outdo' artificial visual systems in resolving ambiguities without using top-down information.

The fact that Marr and his co-workers were unable to implement the object recognition stage of his model could be an indication that bottom-up processing is inadequate as a model of this stage in an artificial vision system: again, it does not necessarily follow that human object recognition relies on top-down influences. Biederman's model certainly gives no space to top-down conceptually-driven processing as a source of correct object descriptions. However, the cascade model, introduced by Humphreys as a convincing explanation for the 'advanced' stages of object recognition, also offers a way of reconceptualizing the earlier stages: any or all of the stages which were laid out, for heuristic reasons, as a sequence of independent stages could be thought of as interacting with one another. The notion that information is 'fed forward' from one stage to a second, *before* the first is complete, suggests an economical way in which input could be processed. It seems particularly likely that Gestalt processes are not confined to simple grouping of elements at one stage of processing, but operate in cascade across several stages of processing. Models such as Biederman's employ Gestalt-like principles (collinearity, symmetry, etc.) in order to derive geons. The cascade model enables us to conceptualize how Gestalt processes might commence within the full primal sketch but spread their influence 'forward' to later processing stages. In short, the cascade model offers a possible way of reinterpreting the organization of all stages in object recognition.

To conclude, studies like those outlined in this part indicate as much what we do not know as what we do know about the complexities of object recognition. Part III will consider the processes involved in recognizing 'objects' of a rather special kind: human faces.

Further reading

BRUCE, V. and GREEN, B.R. (1990) *Visual Perception: Physiology, Psychology and Ecology* (2nd edn), Lawrence Erlbaum Associates. A textbook covering many aspects of vision, and including fairly detailed discussion of some of the theories covered in Part II.

HUMPHREYS, G.W. (ed.) (1992) *Understanding Vision: An Interdisciplinary Perspective*, Blackwell. A useful collection of articles including an excellent account of neuropsychological studies.

MARR, D. (1982) *Vision*, W.H. Freeman. The book in which Marr expands his theories in an accessible form. Destined to become a classic.

CRICK, F. (1994) *The Astonishing Hypothesis: The Scientific Search for the Soul*, Macmillan. A fascinating and provocative book which treats the general problem of our visual awareness of the world as a case study for the explanation of consciousness.

Part III
Perceiving and Recognizing Faces

Vicki Bruce

Contents

1   *Introduction*

Most of the time we interact smoothly with other people, approaching friends, avoiding strangers, and talking appropriately to those people we do know. It is usually only when we experience social embarrassment through a failure of identification, or when we make some change in our life that involves meeting new people, that we notice the processes of social identification that normally we take for granted. Recently, my husband and I moved to a different university, and had to learn a whole new set of colleagues and students at work, as well as neighbours and tradespeople in our new village. We have found it a considerable effort to remember faces and names at the rate we encounter them — our professional interest in the processes of person identification appears to have helped rather little. This part will outline what is known of the processes which normally guide our social lives so effortlessly, but which can lead to embarrassment or bewilderment when they break down.

Parts I and II of this book have outlined what is known about the structure and formation of knowledge about concepts, and about the perceptual processes that allow us to decide that a particular visual pattern is a member of a particular category, such as 'a dog', or 'a chair', or a 'coffee mug'. We can think of the process of visual object recognition as that of assigning a pattern to a conceptual category on the basis of its visible features alone. Our concept of 'dog' may be accessed from a picture showing a four-legged animal with a tail, but the concept may also include the fact that it barks, and a barking sound alone is also enough for us to recognize a dog. The question of the stage at which the visible characteristics that access a concept are combined with other relevant attributes will reappear later in this part (i.e. Section 5), which is concerned with the particularly intriguing case of visual face recognition.

Our ability to recognize faces is interesting in part because it provides an excellent example of discrimination *within* a 'basic level' object category. Part I described Rosch's proposal that objects are naturally categorized at the basic level. When we see a picture of a dog, we tend first to assign it to the basic level category 'dog'. Categorization at the superordinate level 'animal', or the subordinate level 'labrador', appears to be achieved, if at all, after this basic level has been accessed. Part II described Biederman's (1987) theory of recognition-by-components, which specifies the primitives for the visual categorization of objects at the basic level. However, this theory leaves a lot unexplained. Our everyday activities involve frequent, and important, discrimination *within* basic level categories, and this discrimination goes beyond even that captured by the notion of a 'subordinate' level category. We distinguish labradors from alsatians — a subordinate level categorization — but we can find our own labrador among others in the park (i.e. we can recognize different individuals within the same subordinate level category). Similarly, we recognize different makes of car, and our own car in the carpark. Face recognition represents an extraordinary development of this ability.

Just as we categorize dogs or chairs into subordinate categories, so we may categorize faces into different 'subordinate' categories, such as 'baby's face', 'man's face', or 'Japanese face'. We also have some ability to identify individual animals or objects, but in the case of faces this ability to identify individuals is of paramount importance. We can recognize many hundreds, possibly thousands, of faces known in our home town, at college, or through the media. These within-category discriminations involve categorizing *differently* patterns which all share the *same* overall structure. For example, all faces must have eyes, nose and mouth, placed in roughly the same relative locations if they are to play their role in seeing, breathing and eating. As we shall see, perhaps as a result of the demands of face recognition, it appears that the perceptual processes which underly face recognition, and possibly other tasks of within-category recognition, are rather different from those proposed for basic level object recognition.

Face recognition is interesting for other reasons too. First, it is difficult to think of another kind of visual pattern which carries such a variety of different kinds of meaning. The face allows us to identify our friends, to decipher their emotions, and helps us to understand speech and regulate conversation. Somehow the human brain is able to decipher each of these different kinds of meaning, without interference from the others. So, you can recognize your mother whatever expression she is wearing. Conversely, you can recognize an angry expression on any face, whether it is familiar or unfamiliar to you. Here, the term **face recognition** will be reserved for situations where we use the face to identify an individual, and the broader term **face perception** will be used to refer to the whole range of activities where information is derived from the face. The problem of face recognition will be placed within the broader context of face perception, since it is important to know the relationship between different aspects of face processing if we are to understand whether face recognition involves 'special' mechanisms not shared in common with other kinds of object recognition. This is a question that we shall return to in the concluding section of Part III.

SAQ 22
List four different roles that the face plays in interpersonal communication. What attributes or 'features' of the face do you think might be involved in each?

Face recognition is also interesting to psychologists because of its importance in a number of applied settings. Often one of the strongest pieces of evidence to convict a person of a crime is their identification by a witness to that crime. Yet criminal identification is notoriously prone to error, and there have been some remarkable cases of mistaken identity documented in legal history (e.g. see Devlin, 1976). If we understood how we perceive and recognize faces, perhaps identification procedures could be improved. Furthermore, given that the face is the most visible identifying clue to a person, it would be a valuable security aid if we knew enough about face recognition to program computers to search automatically for particular people (perhaps to look out for known terrorists at an airport), or for a robotic security guard to check for known personnel. Understanding how the human brain performs tasks can provide important clues about successful strategies for automation.

In order to make progress in explaining face recognition we need to understand how the human brain processes and stores information about faces and the people to whom they belong. In recent years, we have begun to put together a reasonably clear framework for understanding how this is done. The next section introduces what is known about the perceptual process of describing and representing faces for recognition. In contrast to other kinds of visual patterns, faces seem to be processed configurally, or 'holistically'. Other contrasts between face recognition and basic level object recognition are introduced in Section 3, which shows how surface properties such as skin and hair texture and colour seem to be important for face recognition, whereas outline shape is critical for object recognition. These observations suggest that we need a rather different account of the representation of faces from that of basic level object categorization, and the kind of account that may be needed is considered. Section 4 examines the relationship between the recognition of faces and the analysis of expressions and facial speech, and demonstrates the independence of the information-processing routes which deliver these different kinds of meaning from the face. Section 5 describes what is known about the organization of the cognitive stages involved in person identification, which allow us to know the identity of a familiar face, and to integrate information from the face with that from other routes to person identity. The concluding section addresses the rather tricky question of whether, given what we have learned about face perception and recognition, we should consider faces 'special'.

Summary of Section 1

- Face recognition is theoretically interesting as an example of recognition of individual members within the same 'basic level' category.
- Face perception is involved in many different aspects of social interaction, including expression perception and speech understanding, as well as person identification.
- The identification of people from their faces is important for smooth social interaction, but also in applied contexts such as criminal identification.

2   Features versus configurations: are faces more than the sum of their parts?

2.1   Are face features processed independently?

Part II of this book introduced current theories of basic level object recognition, where scientists such as Marr and Biederman suggest that an object is described as a set of explicit 'primitive' parts (generalized cylinders, or geons) and their spatial arrangement, which together form the structural description of an object's shape. Is this how faces are represented in recognition? Are faces described as a set of parts (which might be the face features — eyes, nose, mouth, for which we have labels) and their spatial arrangement? In recent years, there have been a number of demonstrations that faces seem to be described in a more **configural** or **holistic** way than is captured by this kind of account. However, while several studies suggest that faces are processed more as 'configurations' than as arrangements of independent 'features', there are a number of tricky problems of definition and interpretation.

There has been some confusion in the literature between three rather different interpretations of the term 'configural':

1 'Configural' can mean that the *spatial relationships* between features are as important as the features themselves. This is an interpretation of 'configural processing' which would be quite consistent with the structural description approach already encountered in Part II.
2 'Configural' can mean that face features *interact* with one another (so that the perception of the shape of the mouth, say, is affected by the shape of the nose).

3 'Configural' can mean that faces are processed *holistically* (i.e. they are not analysed into separable features at all).

As we shall see in the evidence reviewed in this section, psychologists now tend to agree that a face is more than just the sum of its parts, but studies of face processing have not always made explicit which sense of 'configural' is under investigation.

This section describes the kinds of experiments which have been used to explore the manner in which face patterns are encoded and stored. To address such questions, psychologists have conducted a number of experiments on the matching or recognition of artificially constructed faces, where different parts of the face can be altered or moved around.

Perhaps because human language has discrete labels for different face features such as 'eyes' and 'mouth', there has been a tendency to assume that, *if* the visual system analyses face patterns in some way that makes their parts explicit, these same features (eyes, nose, mouth, etc.) will form the building blocks of the description. Thus, the prevailing (implicit) assumption has been that a part-based description of the face might comprise a list of face features, each with different specific values (e.g. eyes: *wide*; nose: *long*; lips: *thin*; hair: *curly*, etc.). With this kind of implicit theory, psychologists during the 1970s began to enquire whether face features were indeed processed independently, or whether there was some interaction between different feature values (see the second definition of 'configural' above). Bradshaw and Wallace (1971), for example, constructed faces out of Identikit — a set of varying line-drawn features used by the police to construct images of faces from witnesses' descriptions. They constructed pairs of faces that differed by fixed numbers of features, and explored how quickly volunteers could make the decision that two faces in a pair were different as a function of the number of features that differed. Figure 3.1 overleaf illustrates the kinds of materials used by Bradshaw and Wallace in this experiment. They found that the time taken to make 'different' judgements decreased in proportion to the number of features that differed between two faces. The more differences there were, the faster subjects could respond. From this they concluded that face features were processed independently and in sequence. The more features differed between the two faces, the sooner, on average, subjects would encounter a difference between the two faces if they based their decision on a sequential comparison of the individual components. A number of other studies, reviewed by Sergent (1984), reached similar conclusions.

SAQ 23
Can you think of any other interpretations of this result?

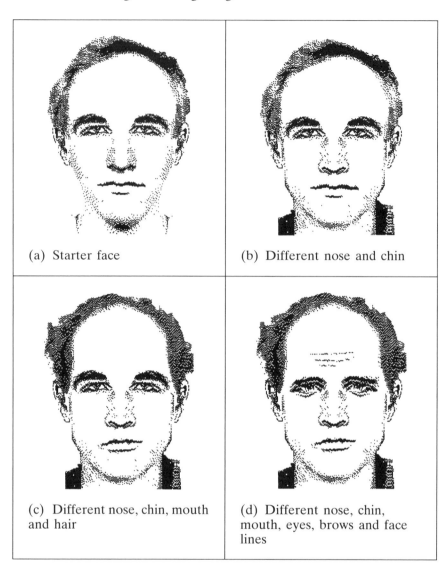

(a) Starter face

(b) Different nose and chin

(c) Different nose, chin, mouth and hair

(d) Different nose, chin, mouth, eyes, brows and face lines

Figure 3.1 Examples of faces similar to those used by Bradshaw and Wallace (1971), made using Mac-a-Mug Pro™ software which allows faces to be constructed from different features on a Macintosh computer. The faces shown illustrate conditions tested in Bradshaw and Wallace's experiment where face pairs could be constructed showing differences in two (a versus b), four (a versus c), or seven (a versus d) facial features

Sergent (1984) noted that, in most experiments where people had explored feature-based processing, faces which differed in several features also differed more in terms of their overall configurations than faces which differed in few features. Thus, the results of such experiments were inconclusive about whether or not the features were processed independently of each other. Sergent (1984) set out to rectify this (see Techniques Box N).

TECHNIQUES BOX N

Interactive Processing of Different Aspects of Facial Appearance
(Sergent, 1984)

Rationale
Sergent reasoned that, if features were processed independently, a 'different' judgement made to faces differing on more than one feature should not be made more quickly than a different judgement made to the fastest of the individual feature judgements alone. This is because a 'different' judgement can be made as soon as any one different feature is spotted. For example, if changes in the shape of the chin were detected more quickly, by all subjects, than any other type of change, then changing something else (e.g. the eyes) in addition to the chin should not speed the decision *unless* there was some kind of interaction between the processing of the chin and that of the eyes.

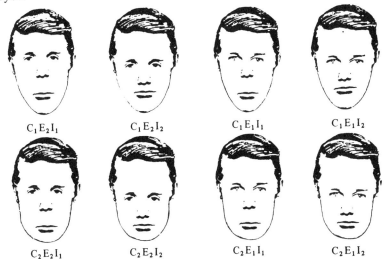

$C_1E_2I_1$ $C_1E_2I_2$ $C_1E_1I_1$ $C_1E_1I_2$

$C_2E_2I_1$ $C_2E_2I_2$ $C_2E_1I_1$ $C_2E_1I_2$

Figure 3.2 The eight different faces used by Sergent (1984) showing each possible combination of two different chins (C1 and C2), two different eye colours (E1 and E2), and two different arrangements of internal space (I1 and I2) (Sergent, 1984, p.226)

Method

Sergent (1984) constructed eight slightly different faces from a 'kit' of face features (see Figure 3.2). All the faces were made from the same features, except that each had one of two different *chins*, two different *eye* colours, and two different arrangements of the internal features (*internal space*). The variation in 'internal space' was created by placing the eyes and nose either relatively high in the face, or relatively low in the face. (The internal space variable could be viewed as a manipulation of a 'configuration' of features, but in this experiment it was treated as a single composite feature.)

   Subjects were shown pairs of faces and asked to decide whether they were the same or different. Faces within a 'different' pair could differ from one another on just one feature (e.g. they could be identical apart from different chins), or on two features (e.g. eyes and chins different), or on all three features. These 'different' pairs were intermixed with other pairs where both faces were identical, and subjects were asked to decide whether each pair of faces was 'same' or 'different' as quickly, but accurately, as possible. The data of interest were the average times taken to make decisions to pairs which had different degrees of difference between them (one, two or three features).

Results

The average time taken to respond 'different' to faces is shown in Table 3.1. The first thing to note is that Sergent confirmed the finding of Bradshaw and Wallace (1971), that the more features differed between faces, the faster a 'different' response could be made. Sergent's results also show that when only a single feature differed between the faces, then 'different' decisions were made most quickly when this difference was between the chins, and this was true for all subjects in the experiment. When Sergent examined how quickly subjects could make a decision when something in addition to the chin was altered, she found that differences were detected more quickly still, which suggested that there was interactive processing of different dimensions of facial appearance.

   This observation was confirmed by more complex statistical analysis which formally revealed an interaction between different face features in some combinations, as suggested by simple inspection of the mean reaction times in Table 3.1 opposite. Error rates (not shown in Table 3.1) were also analysed and similar patterns of effect were found.

Table 3.1   Average time taken to respond 'different' to faces with varying degrees of difference

	Single feature changed	*Two features changed*	*Three features changed*
(a) Mean time in milliseconds (ms) for different numbers of feature changes	832	738	677
(b) Mean time (ms) for different types of feature changes	C E I 750 875 870	C+E E+I C+I 675 867 672	E+C+I 677

C = Chin,   E = Eyes,   I = Internal space

The results of this experiment, along with other studies on the rated similarity of pairs of 'different' faces, led Sergent to conclude that face features are processed interactively — that a configuration emerges from a set of features which is more than the sum of its parts. This is clearly consistent with the second definition of 'configural' listed earlier (see pages 142–3) and perhaps also with the third: the processing advantage shown when more than one feature differs between the faces may imply that, in normal face processing, individual face features are not made explicit at all. Other studies, described later in this section, also support this conclusion.

Interestingly, however, when Sergent repeated her experiment with the face images presented *upside-down*, the results obtained were consistent with a model of *independent* feature processing. With upside-down faces, combinations of feature changes were *not* detected more quickly than the single fastest feature change. This is just one of a number of studies suggesting that the processing of upright and inverted faces differs — it seems that upright faces benefit from interactive or even 'holistic' processing, while the features of upside-down faces are processed independently of one another. Section 2.3 will consider in more detail what the effects of inversion reveal about face processing.

Summary of Section 2.1

- Some early studies suggested that face features might be compared and remembered independently of one another.
- Sergent's (1984) study suggested that upright faces are not processed simply as a set of independent components (face features), but in some more 'interactive', 'configural' or 'holistic' form.

2.2   *Further evidence for configural processing of faces*

Demonstrations such as Sergent's, which illustrate that the dimensions of faces interact, do not really clarify the nature of the 'configural' processing involved. Are the results observed because the perception of one part interacts with that of another, or because the 'parts' are not made **explicit** at all in the visual representation of faces?

A number of recent papers have attempted to address this issue more convincingly. The study we shall examine in detail is that of Tanaka and Farah (1993). (See Techniques Box O.)

TECHNIQUES BOX O

Are Faces Represented in Memory Holistically or as Separate Components? (Tanaka and Farah, 1993)

Rationale
Tanaka and Farah (1993) contrasted the representation of faces as a set of explicit component parts (such as the geons in Biederman's (1987) theory of object recognition — see Part II, Section 6) with representation in a more holistic format. If parts of faces are represented separately and *explicitly* in the description used by the visual system (e.g. nose: *long*; eyes: *large*, etc.), then memory for these parts tested one-by-one in isolation from the face should be as good as memory for the parts when they are embedded in the context of a whole face. If, however, the face is represented in a way that does *not* make individual parts explicit, then memory for the parts in isolation should be at a disadvantage compared with memory for the parts tested in the whole face.

Method

Materials:
The face materials used in the experiments were constructed using the Mac-a-Mug Pro™ software, which was illustrated in Figure 3.1. The specific materials used in Tanaka and Farah's experiments are illustrated in Figure 3.3.

General procedure:
In the experiments, subjects learned proper names for faces constructed from particular combinations of eyes, nose and mouth (e.g. they learned that one particular set of features was called Larry). Later, the experimenters probed subjects' memory for the appearance of the faces they had learned, by asking them to choose between two alternative versions of one of the features that they had learned from each face. For example, they might be asked to choose between two different versions of Larry's nose. One of the versions was the nose that subjects had originally studied, and one was the nose that belonged to a different person's face. To probe their memory

---

for which nose belonged to Larry's face, subjects might either be shown two different alternatives of the *whole* pattern that they had originally learned and asked which one was called Larry, or two different alternatives of the *isolated* feature (in this case, the nose) alone and asked which nose belonged to Larry (see Figure 3.3). The number of correct choices of the nose was compared in the whole face and in the isolated feature condition.

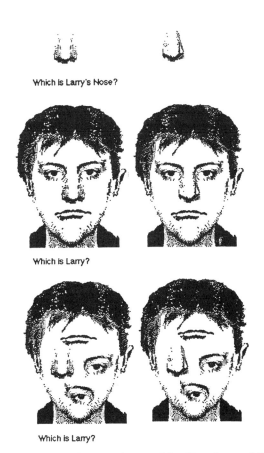

Figure 3.3   Examples of test pairs used by Tanaka and Farah (1993) in Experiment 1. Subjects had learned names to correspond to normal faces, and scrambled faces. At test, they were shown pairs such as these and asked to identify the exact version that belonged to the memorized person. In all three panels, there is a difference in only the nose. In the top panel, isolated noses are tested to probe memory for this difference. In the bottom two panels, memory for the nose is set in the context of the normal face, or scrambled face   (Tanaka and Farah, 1993, p.231)

Experiment 1
Using the above procedure, subjects learned proper names for both normal faces and scrambled faces (in which face features were rearranged). They were then tested for their recognition of different features from the normal faces and scrambled faces, either by presenting the features in isolation, or by presenting them within the contexts where they had been learned (see Figure 3.3).

Results
Table 3.2 shows the percentage of face features which were identified correctly, using the different methods of learning and testing. Tanaka and Farah found that features learned in the context of a normal face were better tested in that context, while those learned in a scrambled face were better tested in isolation.

Table 3.2   Percentage of face features identified correctly, using different methods of learning and testing

	Context in which feature tested:	
	In learning context	*Alone*
Context in which feature learned:		
In normal face	73	62
In scrambled face	64	71

Experiment 2
The experimenters used the same method to compare learning of features from normal upright faces with upside-down faces. For upright faces, they again showed an advantage for testing features in the context of the whole face, but for inverted faces there was no such advantage.

Experiment 3
Upright normal faces were compared with pictures of houses, where memory for 'features' such as windows or doors was tested instead of memory for face features. Again, there was an advantage shown for features of whole faces tested in the context of the face, but for houses it made no difference to recognition accuracy whether the features were tested in a whole house or in isolation.

Tanaka and Farah concluded that the representation of whole faces was based, at least in part, on a holistic description of the images, which led to the superior memory for that face when tested as a whole. This is consistent with the third interpretation of configural processing, according to which faces are not analysed into separate features at all.

In contrast, scrambled faces, upside-down faces and houses seemed to be represented in a way where the component parts *were* represented separately and explicitly in the description. In each case, when memory for the parts of these other patterns was tested, there was no disadvantage when the parts were tested in isolation, and for the scrambled faces the isolated condition was actually better than testing in the original context. These results again suggest that upright faces are processed differently from other kinds of patterns which have similar overall complexity.

Summary of Section 2.2

- Tanaka and Farah investigated whether parts of faces — face features — were made explicit in face representation.
- They found that memory for face features was poorer when tested in isolation than in the context of whole faces, supporting the claim that upright, normally arranged faces are processed holistically without separate explicit representation of parts.
- For other equally complex patterns, such as scrambled faces, upside-down faces and pictures of houses, there was no advantage for testing their parts in the context of the whole pattern. This suggests that these patterns are not processed holistically.

2.3   Differences between the processing of upright and inverted faces

Tanaka and Farah showed that the representation of upside-down faces seems to differ from that of upright faces, because upside-down faces seem to be described as a set of independent components contrasting with the holistic description used for upright faces. Furthermore, the recognition of upside-down faces seems to suffer as a result of this mode of representation.

One of the best established findings in the field of face recognition is that faces are extremely difficult to recognize upside down. Of course, most things get harder to recognize in an unfamiliar orientation, but Yin (1969) compared recognition memory for faces with the recognition of other familiar object categories, such as buildings, and showed that, while faces were recognized *more* accurately than other objects when upright, they were recognized *least* accurately when turned upside down. You can demonstrate this peculiar difficulty for yourself by finding a photograph showing a large set of people familiar to you — perhaps an old school or college photo, or a picture of the guests at your wedding. Turn this upside down and see how difficult it is to recognize the faces.

Since these early experiments by Yin, a number of people have demonstrated that inverted faces seem to be processed differently from upright faces — somehow the different features in an inverted face cannot be integrated to give a coherent impression when the face is inverted.

A particularly convincing demonstration of this was given by Young et al. (1987). They took pictures of well-known faces and sliced them horizontally to form separate upper and lower face halves. They then paired the upper halves with the 'wrong' lower halves. For example, the upper half of Mrs Thatcher's face was paired with the lower half of Shirley Williams' face (at the time, another famous member of parliament). Volunteers were asked to name the top halves of the faces presented in isolation, or when paired with the wrong lower halves. They found that the top halves were much harder to name when they were aligned with different lower halves, compared with a condition where the top halves were shown alone, and a condition where upper and lower halves were misaligned. Their explanation of this effect was that the alignment of the face halves produced a 'new' configuration from the top and bottom features, and they used this to make a further case for the importance of configural processing in face recognition. However, when these composite face images were turned upside down, people were *more* accurate at naming the halves of the faces than they were when the composites were shown upright.

SAQ 24
Why should performance on recognizing halves of upside down composite faces be *superior* to that on upright composite faces in this experiment?

A further compelling illustration of how face processing is affected by inversion is provided by Thompson's (1980) **Thatcher illusion**. Thompson took a picture of Margaret Thatcher, and cut out and inverted the eyes and mouth within the face (see Figure 3.4). When viewed upright the result looked grotesque, but when turned upside down, the picture looked quite normal, and very similar to the original version of the picture.

SAQ 25
Try to think of a possible explanation for this illusion, before reading further.

Bartlett and Searcy (1993) outlined three possible explanations of the Thatcher illusion:

1 *The expression processing hypothesis:* The illusion arises from an impairment in *expression processing*. Because expressions are difficult to recognize upside down, the strange arrangement of the eyes and mouth cannot be interpreted as a grotesque expression when the face is inverted, and therefore it appears near normal.

2 *The reference frames hypothesis:* The illusion arises from the conflict between the *reference frames* against which the orientation of the tops and bottoms of the features can be perceived. One reference frame is provided by the observer's own visual system, the other by the face itself. When the face is upright, the orientation of the tops and bottoms of the inverted features is readily seen since these are inverted with respect to both of these reference frames. When the face is inverted, there is no longer a conflict with the viewer-centred reference frame and so the face appears more normal.

3 *The configural processing hypothesis:* The illusion results from the difficulty in perceiving the *configuration* of face features when a face is inverted. Because the relationship *between* the eyes, nose and mouth is less easy to perceive in an inverted face, the strangeness of the Thatcher face cannot be seen.

Bartlett and Searcy (1993) designed an experiment to see which of these accounts was correct (see Techniques Box P overleaf).

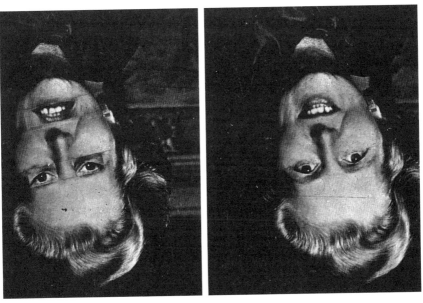

Figure 3.4 The Thatcher illusion. If the faces are viewed upside-down, neither looks particularly odd. If the page is inverted, however, the grotesque expression on one of the Thatcher faces is revealed   (Thompson, 1980)

TECHNIQUES BOX P

Investigating the Thatcher Illusion (Bartlett and Searcy, 1993)

Rationale

To investigate which of the three accounts was correct, Bartlett and Searcy set out to see how 'grotesque' different kinds of faces appeared when shown upright or inverted. They compared subjects' responses to 'Thatcherized' faces, whose features were changed as in the original illusion, faces with grotesque expressions, and faces distorted by having their features moved close together or far apart.

1 According to the expression processing hypothesis, which assumes that expressions are difficult to recognize upside down, faces with grotesque expressions, as well as the Thatcher faces, should appear less grotesque when inverted.

2 According to the reference frames hypothesis, *only* the Thatcher faces should appear less grotesque when inverted, since it is only these faces whose grotesqueness results specifically from the misalignment of top/bottom directions.

3 According to the configural or holistic processing hypothesis, which assumes that inverted faces are not processed configurally, faces distorted by moving features together or apart, as well as the Thatcher faces, should appear less grotesque when inverted.

Method

Several different types of faces were obtained by asking actors to pose different expressions, and the resulting faces were then manipulated using a computer paint package to produce the distorted versions. The following types of face were used:

(a) Thatcherized (i.e. faces where the eyes and mouth were inverted within the face, as in Figure 3.4).

(b) grotesque expressions

(c) neutral expressions

(d) smiling expressions

(e) distorted faces where the location of features was distorted by moving the eyes and mouth within the face.

Subjects were shown several examples of each of these different kinds of faces, both upright and inverted, and asked to rate how 'grotesque' each appeared on a seven-point scale. The results of interest were the mean 'grotesqueness' ratings obtained for each kind of face when upright and when inverted.

Results

The results supported the configural processing hypothesis. Faces with grotesque expressions did *not* look any less grotesque when inverted, but faces whose features had been moved around *did* look less grotesque. Like the Thatcher faces, faces distorted by movement of features appeared more normal when inverted. However, the reduction in grotesqueness was greater for the Thatcherized faces than for the distorted faces (see Table 3.3).

Table 3.3   Mean grotesqueness ratings (7 = most grotesque) for upright and inverted faces of different types (means over different conditions from Bartlett and Searcy, 1993, Table 1)

Face type:	Thatcherized	Grotesque expressions	Distorted features
Upright	6.5	4.7	5.5
Inverted	3.7	4.8	4.4
Difference	2.8	−0.1	1.1

This experiment, along with several others described by Bartlett and Searcy (1993), provides more evidence for the configural processing hypothesis. The Thatcher illusion appears to arise because the components of an inverted face are processed independently of one another. The grotesque appearance of the upright faces arises because of the *relationship between* the arrangements of the eyes and of other parts of the face, which can only be seen with the configural processing mode available for upright faces. Neither the expression processing account nor the reference frame account is consistent with the data.

In Part II, Section 5.3, reference was made to Palmer's work (1992) which showed that a reference frame intrinsic to a pattern or object may provide a basis for an orientation-invariant representation of it. However, we have seen here that the reference frame account does not seem to be a good explanation for the Thatcher illusion. Evidence against the reference frame account of this illusion was also produced by Valentine and Bruce (1985). Such demonstrations do not mean that there is no role played by a head-based reference frame in face perception, merely that this is not the source of this particular illusion.

To sum up, in several different studies it has been demonstrated that the representation of upright faces involves something different from, or additional to, a straightforward structural description in which different types of face feature and their spatial relationships are made explicit.

Are upright faces processed in this configural or holistic way because there is something special about face recognition, or are other categories of objects also discriminated in a similar way? Diamond and Carey (1986) devised an ingenious way to examine this. They tested memory for faces and for dogs in normal subjects and in dog judges and breeders, who are expert at discriminating *within* a different class of objects which share the same overall shape. Diamond and Carey found that the dog experts were also disproportionately affected by inversion of dog pictures in a dog recognition task, compared with non-experts. These results suggest that the importance of the relationship between different parts of a pattern arises as a result of frequent exposure to, and discrimination within, this class of objects. It may be this configural processing which distinguishes novice from 'expert' performance at within-category discrimination. It is interesting to note in this context that Carey (1981) has suggested that young children process faces in a more piecemeal way than older children who process faces more as configurations. Carey (1992) explores this theme further.

What conclusions can we draw from these observations? It appears from the evidence that upright faces are processed rather differently from other kinds of object which people are usually less able to individuate. It may be that the demands of individuating a category whose members all have the same overall structure require a different mode of processing, more capable of encoding the subtle differences which distinguish one individual person from another. Diamond and Carey's dog breeders may also be forced into this alternative processing mode by the demands of within-category discrimination. Generally, then, this processing mode may reflect the acquisition of expertise in a particular domain.

Summary of Section 2.3

- Configural processing is impaired when faces are inverted, and this seems to explain why upside-down faces are so difficult to recognize.
- Bartlett and Searcy's experiment suggested that the 'Thatcher illusion' is also explained by the absence of configural processing of inverted faces.
- This reinforces the conclusion that the processing and recognition of upright faces appears to involve a configural or holistic representation, while that of upside-down faces seems to rely upon representing discrete components.
- Other kinds of 'expert' within-category discriminations also appear to be affected disproportionately by inversion, and may also rely on a configural processing mode when upright.

3   The representational process in face recognition

3.1   The importance of surface properties for face recognition

So far in this part, we have examined at some length evidence suggesting that face recognition seems to involve more configural or holistic processing than the recognition of basic level objects. This section will describe other ways in which the description (i.e. the mental representation) of faces seems to differ from that used for basic level object recognition, and will consider the theoretical implications of these differences. First let's look at the role of colour, shading and texture.

It is an important part of Biederman's theory of object recognition (see Part II, Section 6) that the geons themselves are specified by the layout of edges and junctions obtained from the 'primal sketch'. Surface characteristics such as colour or texture play no role in defining the geons, though Biederman does not deny that they may play a disambiguating role in identifying, say, an orange from a grapefruit. In contrast, however, for face recognition it seems that these surface characteristics play a much more fundamental role. Representations for face recognition seem to preserve information about the lightness and/or colour of the surface (its **pigmentation**), at least crudely. One demonstration of this comes from the effects of **photographic negation**.

Face recognition is dramatically impaired when pictures are presented in photographic negative form (e.g. Galper and Hochberg, 1971; Phillips, 1972). For example, in a recent experiment, Bruce and Langton (1994) compared the effects of negation with those of inverting face images. Subjects were given a list of 28 famous faces, and asked to attempt to identify each face as it appeared for a total of five seconds. Upright positive images were identified correctly in 95 per cent of cases under these conditions. This rate dropped to 70 per cent for inverted, 55 per cent for negated, and 25 per cent for inverted and negated images. Clearly, negation has an effect which can be even more detrimental than that of inversion.

SAQ 26
Can you suggest two possible reasons for the difficulty of recognizing photographic negatives?

If faces were identified via some set of measurements made upon a 'sketch' of the layout of face features, then it is not clear why negating images should have such a dramatic effect. In fact, negation has no adverse effect on the recognition of 2-D drawings of faces, which lack pigmentation or shading. A simple line-drawing of a face is no more difficult to identify in negative than in a positive version (Hayes et al., 1986), though such line-drawings are not recognized well in either version, as we discuss below. It is only when *pigmentation* and *shading* are present in the image that negation has its detrimental effect. A negative image of a face shows a brunette as a blonde, and so the reversal of apparent pigmentation could effectively 'disguise' the identity of the face. Moreover, Ramachandran (1988) has demonstrated how the visual system seems generally to assume a stable direction of lighting, from above the scene. If an area which is shaded when lit from above, such as an eye socket, is portrayed with its pattern of shading reversed as in a photographic negative, this might then be interpreted as a 'hump'. Thus, negating a photograph may make it difficult for the visual system correctly to interpret the three-dimensional shape of the face.

Further evidence for the importance of pigmentation and shading in face recognition arises from an examination of what makes a drawing of a face recognizable. Simple line-drawings of faces convey rather a poor likeness. Davies et al. (1978) compared the identification rates of famous faces presented as monochrome photographs with rates obtained when accurate drawings of the faces were made by tracing around all the major features, wrinkles and so forth. These drawings of faces were very poorly recognized compared with the full photographic images. At first glance, such a result seems strange, since we all know of artists' drawings of faces that seem to convey a good likeness. It seems that the key to producing such a likeness is to preserve at least some information about the shading and/or pigmentation levels, by including some elements of shading in the drawing.

This conclusion was strengthened in a study by Bruce, Hanna et al. (1992) which evaluated the efficacy of line-drawings of faces produced by computer algorithm. The algorithm was originally devised by Pearson and Robinson (1985) in order to solve the problem posed by transmitting images of faces down conventional telephone lines. Such lines have limited capacity and would be overloaded if they had to transmit all the information in full colour images of a moving face. The problem was therefore to transmit information in a 'pared down' form while at the same time preserving the likeness of the faces. Pearson and Robinson's (1985) algorithm produced excellent likenesses of people, almost indistinguishable from those produced by a human artist (see Figure 3.5). Their algorithm comprised two components. The first component produced a sketch of the places where there were significant changes in image intensity — a sketch of the 'edges' present, rather like the primal sketch (see Part II). The second component, called the threshold operator, filled in dark areas in the resulting picture, so that any area which was darker than a certain level of grey in the original image was made black in the drawing. In this way, the resulting drawings conveyed information about pigmentation and shading in addition to information about edges.

Applying Pearson and Robinson's algorithm to pictures of famous faces, Bruce, Hanna et al. (1992) were able to show that the inclusion of this threshold operator contributed greatly to the ease with which subjects recognized the drawings. Computer-generated drawings of

Figure 3.5   Comparison of computer-drawings of faces (right-hand images) with artist drawings of the same faces (left-hand images) (Pearson et al., 1990, p.53)

famous faces which included *both* edges and thresholding were recognized almost as well as original photographic images. Those without the threshold operation were recognized considerably less well. Like the effects of negation, such results suggest that face recognition uses information about shading and pigmentation. This contrasts with basic level object recognition, where line-drawings of objects in which shading and pigmentation are absent can be recognized very easily — indeed, it is only when patients who show deficits in object recognition are tested that photographs can be seen to have an advantage for identification. It therefore seems that face recognition cannot be based upon the same 'edge-based' primitives that will suffice to account for basic level object recognition. The descriptions which form the basis of face representation must be ones which somehow preserve the details of surface pigmentation and/or shading.

Summary of Section 3.1

- Faces are difficult to recognize in photographic negative.
- Negation seems to have its detrimental effect by its reversal of pigmentation and/or shading levels.
- Line-drawings of faces are difficult to recognize unless information about pigmentation and/or shading is preserved in some way.
- It can be concluded that the representations mediating face recognition preserve information about pigmentation and shading.

3.2   Image-based coding of faces

The evidence reviewed above suggests that faces are represented both *holistically* and in a way which preserves information about **surface characteristics** of the images, such as pigmentation and texture. How do these constraints fit with possible models of the representational process?

In Part II, you were introduced to theories of basic level object recognition which were based upon volumetric primitives such as generalized cylinders, or geons. You might like to review Section 6. Biederman's (1987) theory of recognition-by-components was described, in which objects are represented for recognition as a set of geons in particular spatial relationships one to another. In this theory, the spatial relationships between the different geons are as crucial to the identity of the objects as the components themselves. The same geon components can enter into the description of several different objects, depending upon their arrangement. For example, a bucket and a coffee mug can be made from the same two geons. This implies an important role for the first kind of configural effect (described in Section 2.1) in the geon theory. Nevertheless, the geons themselves are represented explicitly as parts, and there is no evidence that the perception of one part interacts with that of a different part. This appears to contrast with the interactive or holistic type of configural effect observed with upright faces in Sergent's (1984) and Tanaka and Farah's (1993) experiments (see Techniques Boxes N and O). Thus, geon-based descriptions make parts explicit in a way which does not seem to be characteristic of human face perception. Furthermore, geon-based descriptions discard information about surface characteristics such as pigmentation and shading, which we have seen seem to play an important role in face descriptions.

There are other problems in applying this type of representational scheme to faces. Faces would all generate a similar description at the level of geons, so this kind of account cannot readily be extended to within-category discrimination between different faces. The geon-based approach is good at representing the difference between objects whose shapes differ, but faces all have very similar shapes at the level of analysis that geons were designed to capture.

A more promising account of face representation may be based upon much lower level properties of the *image*. If actual intensity values ('brightness') at different points in the image, and not just changes in intensity ('edges'), form the basis of the coding scheme, then such an image-based scheme would also show sensitivity to the surface properties which seem to be important in the representation of faces. You will recall from Part II, Section 3.3 that the primal sketch in Marr's theory contained a description of the layout of the intensity *changes* across different regions of the image, but no description of what the actual intensity levels were within particular regions of the image. If Marr's primal sketch stage formed an early stage in the representation of faces, we would have to suggest ways in which information about actual intensity levels could be added back in to the description, probably at the later 2.5D sketch stage. Alternatively, it may be that a rather different account of the primal sketch stage of vision could preserve the necessary information about intensity. Watt and Morgan (1985; see also Watt, 1988) describe MIRAGE, a model of the primal sketch stage in vision which differs in a crucial way from Marr's, preserving some information about regions of relative brightness and darkness. Watt (1992) describes the application of this model of the early stages of vision to the processing of facial images.

Although the evidence we have reviewed suggests that such an image-based scheme may have more promise as an account of face recognition than a scheme such as Biederman's, there are major problems to be solved. A scheme which is based on encoding and storing image properties must have some way of solving the problem of recognizing faces despite variations in size, background and viewpoint, as well as changing expressions, all of which alter the image properties. You will remember, from the discussion in Part II, that both Marr and Biederman provide accounts of object recognition in which the final stages are based on viewpoint independent (object-centred) representations, and it is the process of moving from viewpoint centred to object-centred representation which allows the recognition of objects despite variations in image characteristics. In Biederman's model, most of such problems are solved by the representational process itself. This detects geon characteristics which are independent of viewpoint (see Part II, Section 6.2) and size, from an initial edge-based description.

How can similar invariance to local viewing conditions be achieved with an image-based coding scheme for faces? Human face recognition appears quite tolerant of changes in size and background, at least under some circumstances. This suggests a process of normalizing for size, and selecting figure from ground which would need to be built into a full account of the encoding process. In contrast, however, recognition of pictures of unfamiliar faces suffers quite badly when there is a change in viewpoint between study and test (Bruce, 1982). This suggests that our ability to recognize faces across transformations in viewpoint may arise only as a result of storing multiple representations of a person's face, each corresponding to the face seen from a different viewpoint. It may be that face recognition is achieved by viewpoint dependent rather than object-centred representations, which would be a further contrast between the processes of face recognition and basic level object recognition.

SAQ 27
There are a number of situations where it might be desirable if machines could be used to recognize faces for security reasons. List some of these situations, and consider for each of your chosen examples whether problems of changing viewpoint, size, lighting or background would need to be overcome.

Summary of Section 3.2

- Representations for face recognition seem more likely to be based on an analysis of image properties than on an edge-based system such as geons.
- Image-based coding schemes will require some way of achieving invariance across variations in superficial characteristics such as size or background, as well as changes in viewpoint, expression and lighting.

162

3.3   Distinctiveness and caricature

We are clearly some way from deciding what representational scheme is used by the human visual system in face identification, though the evidence favours some possibilities more than others. One further set of findings that the eventual theory must be able to explain are the effects on face recognition of the 'distinctiveness' of faces.

Faces are not all equally easy to recognize. Faces which other people regard as 'distinctive' or atypical in appearance can be recognized more accurately or more quickly than those which are rated as more typical in appearance. This is true even for highly familiar faces. A face with an unusual appearance, such as Ronald Reagan, is recognized as familiar more quickly than one which is more typical in appearance, such as John Major (Valentine and Bruce, 1986a,b). Thus, discrimination of individual identity is facilitated by a distinctive appearance.

SAQ 28
How do these results obtained with faces compare with the typicality effects found in the concept representation literature (see Part I, Section 3.2)?

At first glance, we have here another contrast with basic level object recognition, where typical members enjoy an advantage over distinctive or atypical ones (see Part I, Section 5.1). Valentine and Bruce (1986b) set out to investigate this contrast systematically, by seeing how the typicality and distinctiveness of faces affected individual identification (is this face familiar?) compared with basic level classification of the face as a kind of object (is this pattern a face?). Their experiment is outlined in Techniques Box Q.

TECHNIQUES BOX Q

Recognition of 'Typical' and 'Distinctive' Faces
(Valentine and Bruce, 1986b)

Rationale
The aim was to compare the processing of faces rated as distinctive in appearance with those rated as more typical in appearance in tasks requiring access to representations of individual faces (is this person familiar?) or tasks requiring access only to the basic level category of faces (is this a face?).

Method

Pretest:
Subjects were shown pictures of familiar (i.e. famous) and unfamiliar faces and asked to rate each face for 'how well it would stand out in a crowd, for example when being met at a railway station'. Instructions

---

stressed that ratings should be made on the basis of appearance, not fame. The faces were allocated to a 'distinctive' group or a 'typical' group on the basis of subjects' ratings.

Familiarity task:
A new group of subjects were shown a random sequence of the faces from the pretest and asked to decide, as fast as possible for each face, whether it was familiar or not.

Categorization task:
Subjects were shown examples of faces from the pretest interspersed with 'jumbled' non-faces in which the positions of internal features were rearranged (e.g. mouth located above nose). For each pattern, subjects were asked to decide, as fast as possible, whether it was a face or non-face.

Results
In the face *familiarity* task, responses were made more quickly to famous faces in the distinctive group than those in the typical group (see Table 3.4). There was no difference in times to respond to the unfamiliar faces. In the face/non-face categorization task, responses were made more quickly to the famous faces in the typical group (see Table 3.4), a result which was also found with unfamiliar faces. Similar results have been found when the familiar faces used were personally familiar (faces from the subjects' own university department).

Table 3.4   Decision times (milliseconds) to distinctive and typical famous faces (data from Experiments 1 and 2, Valentine and Bruce, 1986)

	Distinctive	*Typical*
Average time to decide that faces were familiar	661	707
Average time to decide that faces were faces	608	561

These findings show that when recognition at the basic level is required, faces show the same effects found for other objects — typical exemplars are classified as faces more easily.

Results from a different experiment (Valentine and Endo, 1992) showed that this same pattern of effects is found even when faces must be classified at the subordinate level. When subjects were asked to categorize faces as Japanese or Caucasian they were faster to categorize the faces rated as typical of each ethnic group than to categorize exemplars which were rated as more distinctive in appearance. However, when discrimination of individual *identity* is required, as in the familiarity task in Techniques Box Q, then the opposite effect is found, and distinctive items enjoy the advantage.

Valentine (1991) explains these results by appealing to a multidimensional **face space**, where each dimension is a physical dimension along which face appearance varies. Dimensions of the space could be things like hair colour, face shape, or width of lips, or more abstract or holistic properties of face images. It does not matter for present purposes. On this account, a face is represented by its location in the multidimensional space of variation, and so most faces having values on these dimensions which are similar to those of many other faces will cluster together in face space. This is similar to Rosch's typical feature model (see Part I, Section 4.1), in which typical exemplars share many of the characteristic features of the category and atypical (distinctive) items share few of them. In Valentine's model, it is the *values* of features (e.g. hair: *brown*; eyes: *blue*) which are shared by typical exemplars and not by atypical exemplars. A face with very unusual values on dimensions — for example, an elderly male face with long, straight, white, blonde hair (e.g. Jimmy Saville) — would be located in a part of the space shared with few if any other faces. If the task of face identification involves locating an individual exemplar within the space, it can be seen that this must be easier if the face is located in an empty region of space, since there will be few other faces to compete for identification. However, if the task is to decide whether the item is a member of the category 'face', it is then going to be advantageous if the exemplar falls within the region of space shared by lots of other faces.

Valentine's model implies that faces which are distinctive in appearance should be more deviant on a number of physical dimensions than more typical faces. Bruce et al. (1994) have recently measured a large set of faces and confirmed that distinctive faces do have more deviant measurements on features such as nose width, hair length, etc. than faces rated as more typical in appearance, a finding consistent with Valentine's model.

Moreover, it can be shown that making a face *more* distinctive in appearance can enhance its identification. This appears to be the basis for caricature, where an artist exaggerates and distorts a person's true appearance and yet seems to convey the essence of their identity. Recent work on computer-created caricatures has shown that caricatures can be created effectively by applying a transformation that increases the difference between a given face and an 'average' face. Caricaturing a simple outline drawing of a face in this way makes it much more recognizable (Rhodes et al., 1987). Recent advances in computer graphics mean that it is now possible to use a similar technique to make a caricature of a full colour photograph of a person, and Benson and Perrett (1991) have shown that caricatures created automatically in this way can be more recognizable than the original images of the people. This provides an interesting exception to the claim made in Section 3.1 that line-drawings of faces are difficult to recognize in the absence of information about pigmentation and shading. In the case of caricature, the exaggeration of features compensates for the absence of this other information.

Summary of Section 3.3

- Distinctive faces are easier to identify than typical faces.
- Typical faces are more easily classified as faces than distinctive faces.
- Valentine (1991) has accounted for such effects using a model of 'face space' where distinctive faces are represented in more remote and sparsely populated regions.

3.4   Similarities and differences between face recognition and basic level object identification

Sections 2 and 3 of this part have described some apparent differences between the representational processes which seem to be involved in the description of faces, compared with those used for recognizing objects. Before reading further, see if you can remember all the points of difference, or contrast, between the recognition of faces and objects.

The major points we discussed are:

1 Upright faces seem to be processed 'configurally' (probably without their features being made explicit), while the representations employed in processing other objects (e.g. houses) seem to involve explicit parts processed independently of one another.
2 Face recognition seems to be disrupted disproportionately by inversion.
3 Simple line-drawings of faces are poorly identified, unless information about relative light and dark areas is preserved. Outline drawings of objects are readily identified at the basic level.
4 Identification of distinctive faces is better than more typical ones, but typical objects are recognized more easily than distinctive ones at the basic level.

To what extent do these differences reflect fundamental differences between the processing of faces and objects, and to what extent do the differences reflect the different demands of discriminating within rather than between categories?

Taking each of the points of difference above, we saw in Section 2.3 that Diamond and Carey found that dog recognition was affected by inversion in the same way as face recognition when people were expert at dog perception, perhaps because experts processed dogs, as well as faces, in configural mode when upright. As for the identification of line-drawings, we simply do not know how well or badly simple outlines would serve for the identification of individual members of object categories as there is no relevant data. However, Price and Humphreys (1989) have produced some evidence that where individual members of an object category are structurally similar, their identification is influenced by surface properties such as texture and colour. In these terms, faces might just represent a category where members are all structurally similar one to another. As for the advantage of distinctive over typical members for within-category identification, while we do not have data from other object categories, it seems highly likely that if your task is to identify your own dog, your own suitcase or your own car, it will probably be easier if their appearance makes them distinctive compared with other members of the category. (Think of the task of retrieving your suitcase from the luggage reclaim point at an airport.)

Furthermore, in the same way that making faces more distinctive by caricaturing them can enhance their identification, Rhodes and McLean (1990) have shown that, for expert birdwatchers, the identification of line-drawings of individual members of a familiar class of birds was faster if these were caricatured. No such advantage was found for non-experts at bird perception. These findings, alongside those of Diamond and Carey on the inversion effect, suggest that the 'configural' mode of processing may emerge for the 'expert' identification of members of a category sharing the same overall structure, and may not be exclusive to face recognition. Combined with Price and Humphreys' (1989) observations on the importance of surface properties for the recognition of members of structurally similar categories, this suggests that there may be an alternative mode of processing and representing patterns which arises as a result of the demands of discriminating within categories in order to identify individual items whose overall shapes are similar. This alternative mode of processing, which may rely more on image properties than on edge properties, may co-exist with the kind of representational mode used to differentiate objects into basic level categories.

4   Recognizing facial expressions and facial speech

4.1   Introduction: representational demands of expression and facial speech processing

Sections 2 and 3 have concentrated on the more 'visual' side of face perception, in considering the representational processes that underly face recognition. Section 5 will examine the relationship between these visual processes and the retrieval of associated semantic and verbal information about the identity of familiar faces, and describe models of the stages of this full-scale **person identification**. Before we do this, however, we shall look in this section at the relationship between the different uses made of information from face patterns.

In recent years there has been considerable progress in developing cognitive models of person identification. To make this progress it has been important to clarify the relationship between the identification of people from their faces and the other uses made of facial information in interpersonal communication. We now know that face identification, **facial expression analysis** and **lipreading** appear to proceed *independently* of each other, whereas the component stages of person identification appear to be related and to proceed in sequence. This section will consider how converging evidence from different experimental and neuropsychological methods has been used to suggest that there are independent routes for the derivation of different kinds of meaning from the face. First, let's look briefly at the differing perceptual demands of identification, expression analysis and lipreading.

Sections 2 and 3 have focused on trying to understand the perceptual processes that allow us to represent faces in a way which is sufficient for the demands of face identification, where the challenge is to discriminate between many similar individuals. However, we also categorize faces via their expressions, eye-gaze and facial lip movements. It is not necessarily the case that these tasks require the same kind of representational solution.

Take the case of interpreting facial expressions. Here, there appears to be a universally appreciated but relatively *small* set of categories into which face expressions can be assigned. Work by Ekman and associates (see Ekman, 1982) suggests that adults can reliably categorize pictures of posed emotional expressions into about seven categories (happiness, sadness, fear, surprise, anger, disgust/contempt, and interest). Moreover, a variety of literate and preliterate peoples appear to interpret expressions in this same way. The demands of a system needing to distinguish just seven expressions are very different from one needing to distinguish hundreds or thousands of individual identities. It is quite conceivable that a simple set of schematic postures of major face features could suffice for the purposes of expression categorization. Similarly, the visual information which proves useful for lipreading (also known as **facial speech**) is relatively simple, and much of what we read from the lips involves whether and by how much the lips are open. The shape of the lips could again be specified as a relatively straightforward set of parameters derived from a schematic represent-ation of the major face features. Summerfield (1979) showed that lumin-ous lips seen in the dark served remarkably well for lipreading, which suggests that just the changing shape of the lips over time conveys a good deal of what is needed for this task.

This discussion is an example of Marr's claim that we need to under-stand the overall function that a representation needs to serve (the computational level) as well as the algorithms needed to achieve this representation (the algorithmic level). The different demands of differ-ing face perception tasks may be achieved by quite different represen-tational routes. As will be indicated in Section 4.2, there is strong evidence that the routes *are* independent from one another.

4.2   Independent processing of facial expressions and facial identities

The task of recognizing individual identity from a face is *logically* sepa-rate from that of recognizing an emotional expression from a face. In the first case, the requirement is to recognize an individual irrespective of the expression shown on the face. In the second, the task is to recognize an emotional expression (happiness, say) irrespective of other aspects of the facial appearance (e.g. whether it is the face of someone who is old or young, fat or thin).

Consistent with this logical independence, there is converging evi-dence from several different sources that face expressions are pro-cessed independently from face identification. First, experiments with adults have shown that identity seems to be ignored in the classifica-tion of emotional expressions. Bruce (1986) and Young et al. (1986a) each showed that expressions were classified no more quickly when the faces shown were familiar than when they were unfamiliar.

A second source of evidence for the independence of expression identification and person identification arises from studies of neuropsy-chological impairments. As a (rare) result of brain injury, people may be left unable to recognize familiar faces, including those of their spouse, relatives and friends. This condition is termed **prosopagnosia**. The deficiency is a problem of face processing, not memory, since it can be

169

shown that their knowledge of these same familiar people is intact when probed by another route — for example, by asking about the person by name. While some prosopagnosic patients are unable to do very much at all with visual information from faces (one such case will be discussed in Section 4.3), several others have been reported who cannot recognize faces but are quite normal at deriving other kinds of meaning from the face, including identifying emotional expressions (e.g. see Bruyer et al., 1983). So, prosopagnosic patients can often identify emotional expressions normally. In contrast, some patients with a kind of dementia have been reported to find it difficult to recognize emotional expressions, while remaining able to classify famous faces into occupational categories (which requires knowledge of personal identity) (Kurucz and Feldmar, 1979; Kurucz et al., 1979).

SAQ 29
Is there neuropsychological evidence of a double dissociation (see Part II, Section 2.3) between the processing of identity and facial expressions?

Finally, there is evidence from the neurophysiological study of face processing by single cells of the monkey brain that identities and expressions may be processed separately. Research in a number of different laboratories has demonstrated that cells in a particular brain area called the **temporal lobe** respond selectively to faces, just as cells at earlier stages in the visual system respond selectively to simple features such as edges or colours (e.g. see Gross, 1992; Rolls, 1992; Heywood and Cowey, 1992; Perrett et al., 1992). Some of the 'face' cells that have been studied seem additionally to be selective for particular facial identities, responding most strongly when the face shown is that of a particular person known to the monkey. Other cells, in a slightly different brain area, respond selectively to particular facial expressions, irrespective of the person whose face is shown wearing the expression (Hasselmo et al., 1989). Thus, the separation of these functions in the monkey cortex gives further evidence that face recognition and expression perception proceed independently.

Summary of Section 4.2

- There is converging evidence for independent routes for expression perception and face identification from the following three sources:
  - (a) Adults' decisions about expression are no easier for familiar faces than for unfamiliar faces.
  - (b) Some prosopagnosic patients process expressions normally, and some dementing patients appear impaired in expression recognition but not face identification.

(c) Physiological evidence from studies of monkeys suggests the existence of different brain areas, with cells selectively responsive to facial identity and facial expression respectively.

4.3   Facial speech processing

Facial speech processing (i.e. lipreading) is an activity that most of us think is used only by people who have impaired hearing. In fact, there is very good evidence that all of us make use of visual information from the face when deciphering speech. Anecdotally, you may notice that it is very difficult to give your postal code over the telephone without spelling out what the letters stand for ('T for tango'), yet people do not have this difficulty when interacting face to face. Some phonetic distinctions, such as the difference between an 'em' and an 'en' sound, are difficult to hear, but easy to see — 'em' involves lip closure but 'en' does not. You may also notice how disconcerting it is to watch a film with poorly dubbed speech: this shows that we do attend to lip movements and that processing is disrupted when they are not synchronized with speech sounds. A more formal demonstration of the use of lip-read information in interpreting speech sounds is provided by the **McGurk effect** (see Techniques Box R).

TECHNIQUES BOX R

The McGurk Effect (McGurk and McDonald, 1976)

Rationale
If normal speech perception involves the use of visual as well as acoustic information, then it should be possible to bias speech perception by altering the visual information accompanying the acoustic signal.

Method
Adult speakers were filmed as they spoke simple nonsense words such as 'baba', 'gaga', 'papa' and 'kaka'. The films were then edited so that different acoustic events were dubbed on to the visual record of these speech sounds. The voice sound 'baba' was dubbed on to the visual record of the lips saying 'gaga' (and vice versa), and the voice 'papa' dubbed on to the visual presentation of 'kaka' and vice versa. The resulting tapes were shown to children and adults who were asked to report what they heard. It was first established that the sounds were perceived correctly when presented without accompanying faces.

Results

Almost all adults, and most children, were influenced by the visual information when reporting what they 'heard'. For example, when voice said 'baba' and lips said 'gaga' the percept was usually 'dada' — an apparent fusion of information from the two sources. This effect is known as the McGurk effect. With the reverse combination, percepts were usually mixed (e.g. 'bgabga' might be reported). Similar effects were found with the other syllable combinations.

Moreover, Green et al. (1991) showed that the McGurk effect was not reduced if the faces were of males and the voices of females, or vice versa, compared with the usual condition where faces and voices match. This suggests that the processes of audio-visual speech integration are quite independent of those to do with establishing information about a person's identity.

SAQ 30
Suppose that McGurk tapes were made up from famous faces and famous voices, such that faces and voices could match (e.g. Margaret Thatcher's face and voice) or mismatch (e.g. John Major's face and Margaret Thatcher's voice). What prediction would you make about the relative incidence of McGurk effects in these two conditions?

We have seen that studies of the McGurk effect have established that visual information from the face is combined with acoustic information from the voice when perceiving speech, and Green et al.'s (1991) study suggests that this process is independent of other aspects of face processing. Stronger, converging evidence for the independence of facial speech processing from other kinds of face processing has been obtained from a double dissociation observed neuropsychologically.

Campbell et al. (1986) described two patients. The first was a prosopagnosic patient who had difficulty with many aspects of face processing. In contrast to some of the patients discussed above, this lady was uncertain about the sex of faces, could not identify emotional expressions, and failed to identify the vast majority of faces that should have been familiar to her from the media and from her everyday life. However, the patient showed a normal ability to identify speech sounds from still photographs of faces shown mouthing different sounds, and when tested on the McGurk effect showed the same pattern as normal adults. Thus, the patient appeared to process faces normally for speech, despite failing to retrieve any of the other kinds of information that normal people can derive from faces. Her deficits were contrasted with those of a second patient, who presented with word recognition difficulties, not face recognition difficulties. The second patient was quite normal at face processing tasks, *except* those involving facial speech.

She was impaired at recognizing speech sounds from photographs of faces, and showed no McGurk effect. This patient reported what she heard, uninfluenced by what she saw. Interestingly, this double dissociation was maintained even when pictures showing only the lower halves of faces were shown. Thus, the first patient could not say that a smiling mouth was happy, but knew that pursed lips said 'p', while the second knew that a smiling mouth was happy but failed to make normal use of lip shapes in speech perception.

Summary of Section 4.3

- The McGurk effect illustrates that we use lip shapes when interpreting speech sounds.
- The McGurk effect appears to be unaffected by whether face and voice match in gender, suggesting that lipreading proceeds independently of other kinds of categorization of faces.
- Consistent with this, Campbell et al.'s (1986) study shows a double dissociation between lipreading and other uses of facial information in neuropsychological patients.

5 Models for recognizing people

5.1 Stages of person identification

So far, we have contrasted the processing of expression and lipreading with that involved in person identification, and described the evidence that suggests that *independent* information-processing routes are used to deliver different kinds of meaning derived from the face. This independence means that we can consider the nature of the processes which lead to the recovery of identity without worrying about all the other kinds of ways in which faces are meaningful in social interaction. We now turn to consider the details of the sub-processes which lead to full-scale person identification from the face. The complete identification of a known face requires not just that we recognize the pattern of the face as a familiar one, but that we know the context in which we have encountered the person and are able to retrieve their names. Studies of normal adults and brain-injured patients have suggested that there is a sequence of distinct stages involved in retrieving the identity of a person, with failures at each of the different stages characterized by different problems of identification. Hay and Young (1982) first outlined a model of the stages of person identification, and Young et al. (1985) gathered further evidence for this proposal through their investigation of everyday failures in person identification (see Techniques Box S).

TECHNIQUES BOX S

Diary Study of Errors of Everyday Identification
(Young et al., 1985)

Rationale

Young et al. (1985) explored the component processes of person identification by exploring what kinds of errors or difficulties were experienced in everyday life.

Method

Twenty-two volunteers were asked to keep a diary record, over a period of eight weeks, of all those cases where they experienced a difficulty or failure in their ability to recognize someone they knew, whether in the flesh or on the media. They were asked to note certain details about the incident, such as whether the person appeared in an unfamiliar context, and how the incident was resolved. The diary records were then analysed and events of similar types grouped together. The diaries included incidents of failures or difficulties of person identification not involving the face (e.g. failing to recognize the voice of a friend on the phone). Here, only results relevant to face processing will be considered.

Results

Some types of error or difficulty were relatively common, particularly the following:

1 A person was not recognized (e.g. the diarist walked past someone they knew, who then accused them of ignoring them).
2 A person seemed familiar only (e.g. the diarist knew that an encounter was with someone they had met before, but couldn't think why they were familiar).
3 A person was identified but their name could not be retrieved (e.g. the diarist knew that the person on TV was a Scottish Labour politician, but couldn't recall the name).
4 A person was misidentified. Sometimes unfamiliar people were wrongly identified as familiar, and sometimes a familiar person was identified wrongly.

Of even greater significance was the observation that certain error types did *not* occur. For example, no occasion was recorded where the diarist recognized someone as familiar, and knew the name of the person, but could not remember anything else about them.

Young et al. also noted that a frequent occurrence, which was in no way an error, was for people to notice strong resemblances between unfamiliar people and others that they knew (e.g. the subject saw someone who looked just like their father).

Young et al.'s study involved volunteers keeping careful records for several weeks, but you might like to conduct a miniature version of this study by noting down all your own difficulties in person identification for a period of a week or so. See if you can notice examples of the types of errors which were reported in the more extended study.

The pattern of errors and difficulties obtained by Young et al. supported Hay and Young's (1982) proposal that information about personal identity was retrieved in a sequence, and that failure could occur at any stage of the sequence. After representational processing in Young et al.'s model (see Figure 3.6), information about the face of the person encountered is processed by 'recognition units'. These units contain stored representations of known faces. If the face currently being viewed matches one of these representations, information about the resemblance is signalled to the **person identity nodes (PINs)** where basic information about personal identity is stored, and via which names and other details of identity are accessed (from the 'additional information stores'). Decisions about whether or not a particular face is familiar, or

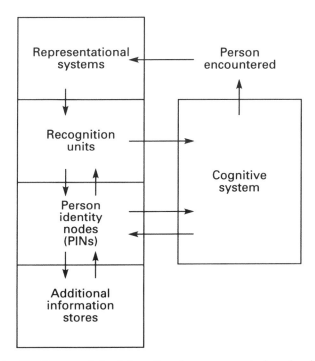

Figure 3.6 Outline model of functional components involved in person identification   (Young et al., 1985, p.518)

about the identity of the person, are made as a result of communication between these levels and the 'cognitive system'. If visual processing fails to deliver a representation of the face which matches one stored in the recognition units, recognition will fail and the person will go unrecognized (error type 1 in Techniques Box S). If the activity is sufficient at the level of the recognition units, but for some reason the retrieval of information via the PINs fails, then the person will seem familiar only (error type 2). If there is a block in the access to the additional information stores from the level of PINs, then the person may be recognized and some information about identity retrieved, but the name (or other details) will not be accessed (error type 3). If the visual representation of a face triggers the wrong recognition unit, then a face may be misidentified (error type 4). Finally, because decisions about whether faces were familiar (and, if so, the basis for this feeling of familiarity) relied upon an interplay between the different identification 'modules' and the rest of the cognitive system, the feelings of resemblance so often noted by the diarists could be explained. For example, on seeing a person who resembled Prince Charles, other information about context — the subject was in their local launderette at the time — would be available via the cognitive system to allow the resemblance signal to be evaluated, and to reduce the likelihood of misidentification.

Further evidence consistent with the sequence of stages on the route to identification (familiarity — personal identity — names) has been obtained in experiments which investigate how quickly subjects can retrieve information of different sorts from the face. A number of experiments have shown that subjects are faster to decide whether a face is familiar than to decide whether or not it is a politician, and faster to make decisions about occupation than ones that require name retrieval (e.g. Young et al., 1986b). Decisions which require that names are accessed are made more slowly than those requiring access to other kinds of personal information, even when the task demands are carefully matched and faces are well learned during the course of the experiment. For example, Johnston and Bruce (1990) showed that subjects were slower to decide whether two faces shared the same first name (both called 'John' or both called 'James') than to decide whether two faces belonged to two people who were both dead, or both alive. This is a somewhat counterintuitive finding, as one might predict that more mental effort is required to decide that John Lennon and John Kennedy are both dead than to decide that they are both called John. Such a result could be explained in terms of a model like that shown in Figure 3.6, if answers to the 'dead or alive' question could be given from information stored at the person identity nodes, but answers about names required access to the additional information stores.

Neuropsychological evidence is also consistent with the idea that there is a sequence of operations establishing face familiarity, retrieving information about identity, and retrieving names. Prosopagnosic patients seem to fail at the first of these stages. Almost all faces appear unfamiliar to the prosopagnosic patient. A different type of patient finds faces familiar, but can retrieve no further information about why the face is familiar. De Haan et al. (1991) describe ME, an amnesic patient, who could correctly decide which of a set of faces was familiar, but had no recollection of why each one was familiar. There seemed to be no way of getting beyond the stage where familiarity was established. Finally, some patients with language difficulties have been described who seem to have a peculiar difficulty in retrieving people's names. Everybody has some problems with retrieving names, especially as they get older, but some neuropsychological patients have much more severe difficulties. Flude et al. (1989) describe EST, an aphasic patient, who performed normally at recognizing famous faces and giving information about such things as the occupations and nationalities of such faces, but failed to retrieve names for the majority of faces which were otherwise well described. For example, when shown John Wayne's face, EST's response included the following: 'I know who he is. Dead. He's a . . . he's a . . . he's an American . . . the last time I saw him he was on the cow, one of the cow pictures.' This patient clearly knew that the person was a dead, American film star, famous for cowboy films, but was quite unable to retrieve the name 'John Wayne'.

Summary of Section 5.1

- Evidence from everyday errors, experiments and neuropsychology suggest that information about personal identity is retrieved via a sequence of stages.
- The stages allow the access of information about familiarity, general information about identity, and finally specific information in the form of the name.
- The sequence of stages required for full identification was expressed as a cognitive model of person identification by Young et al. (1985).

5.2   The Bruce and Young model

Bruce and Young (1986) described a broad functional model of face recognition, which put the stages of person identification described in Section 5.1 into the broader context of their relationship with the other uses made of facial information (see Section 4). The resulting model was a synthesis of a number of theoretical suggestions that had been made earlier by Young and colleagues (e.g. Hay and Young, 1982; Young et al., 1985), and others in the UK (e.g. Bruce, 1979; Ellis, 1986) and beyond (Rhodes, 1985). The model, which is shown in schematic form in Figure 3.7, comprises a number of different processing 'modules' linked in sequence or in parallel. Independent routes are drawn for the processing of emotional expressions, lipreading (termed 'facial speech' by Bruce and Young), and identification. The route labelled 'directed visual processing' was suggested to allow for certain kinds of operations to be performed on faces without accessing identities — for example, looking out for people with white hair when you go to the station to meet your granny (Bruce, 1979). By including the distinct routes for expression analysis, facial speech and directed visual processing, the Bruce and Young model incorporated routes for the processing of information from unfamiliar as well as familiar faces. The route by which familiar faces are identified involves separate stages of representation of the face image (termed 'structural encoding' by Bruce and Young), access of stored structural descriptions of known faces (in **face recognition units — FRUs**), access of information about personal identity (via 'person identity nodes' — PINs), and, finally, retrieval of proper names. Thus, the identification route proposed by Bruce and Young (1986) was very similar to that of the Young et al. (1985) account we considered earlier (see Figure 3.6).

Though broad, the model has the essential attribute of being potentially falsifiable, as illustrated by the following scenario. Suppose you are playing a game of Trivial Pursuit, and are asked to name an actor from a description such as 'Who played the nervous man with the knife in Hitchcock's *Psycho*?'. Imagine that you know the actor's name and find yourself with it on the tip of your tongue, but are unable to retrieve it.

SAQ 31
According to the Bruce and Young model, if you know the identity of the person from a description, and know, but cannot retrieve the name, what kind of clues should help you to retrieve the name? If you are shown a picture of the person, should this help? If you are shown the initials of the name, should this help?

An experiment investigating this sort of situation is described in Techniques Box T on page 180.

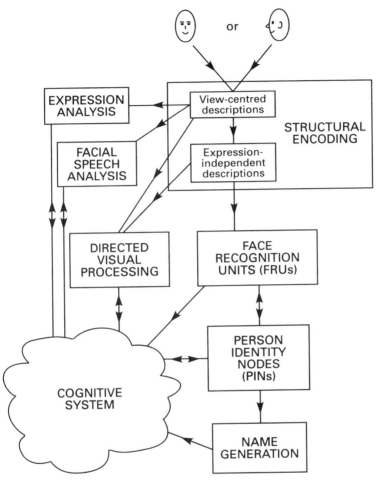

Figure 3.7   A functional model for face recognition   (Bruce and Young, 1986, p.312)

TECHNIQUES BOX T

Investigating the Tip-of-the-Tongue State for Names of People
(Brennen et al., 1990)

Rationale

Brennen et al. (1990) set out to see whether subjects in a **tip-of-the-tongue (TOT)** state, after being asked to identify someone from a description, could be helped to retrieve the name by viewing a picture of the person. The method used built upon that of an earlier investigation by Hanley and Cowell (1988).

Method

Brennen et al. (1990) constructed a series of questions, like those in Trivial Pursuit, which required subjects to retrieve the names of famous celebrities. On those trials where subjects indicated that the required name was on the tip of their tongue, they investigated what happened when the subjects were shown a picture of the person's face. They compared what happened when a picture was shown with what happened when the same question was simply repeated again, on the grounds that a second attempt at retrieving the name might itself relieve the name block. In a second experiment, they compared these two conditions (shown picture, repeat question) with a third condition where the initials of the missing name were shown.

Results

Showing the initials allowed about half of the missing names to be retrieved, but showing a picture of the face did not allow any more names to be produced than simply repeating the question (see Table 3.5). The picture condition and the repeated question condition each led to correct naming in only a small proportion of the TOT states in each of two experiments. Thus, there is no evidence that seeing the face can help retrieve the name in such a situation. Indeed, subjects became annoyed when they were shown the picture of the person whose name eluded them: 'I know what s/he looks like, I just can't remember the name!'

Table 3.5   Percentage of TOT conditions which were resolved by presenting different types of prompts

	Repeat question	*Show picture of face*	*Show initials*
Expt 1	15	12	not tested
Expt 2	11	15	47

The pattern of results was as predicted by the Bruce and Young account. When subjects know that they can identify the person, but experience a name block, they must be at the stage of person identity nodes but unable to get to the next stage of name retrieval. Seeing the face should not help, since there are no direct links between faces and names, and the face should not therefore be able to get them further than the stage at which they are already stuck. Seeing the initials, however, provides partial cues which should facilitate the retrieval of the missing name. The model's predictions were thus upheld in this experiment.

The Bruce and Young model therefore proved robust to such attempts to test it by falsification. Nevertheless, at the time this model was published, a number of findings were emerging that appeared more troublesome for models of this kind. There is not sufficient space here to go into details of all these issues, so a single example, that of 'covert' recognition, will be elaborated.

One of the most difficult problems for the Bruce and Young (1986) model (as well as for the earlier ones of Hay and Young, 1982, and Young et al., 1985) is the observation of **covert recognition** in some prosopagnosic patients. Bauer (1984) showed that prosopagnosic patients with no overt recognition of famous faces showed distinct autonomic responses (in the form of galvanic skin responses — the basis of the 'lie detector' test) when they saw faces that should have been familiar to them. It was as though part of their nervous system recognized the face, but that awareness of this familiarity did not reach the part responsible for conscious report. Such dissociations between unconscious and conscious information processing are fascinating and counterintuitive, and readers are referred to a number of further demonstrations in domains other than face processing (e.g. see Weiskrantz, 1988, for examples of blindsight and other such phenomena). Building on this finding, De Haan, Young and their colleagues set out to see whether covert recognition could be demonstrated using purely behavioural techniques (see Techniques Box U).

TECHNIQUES BOX U

Covert Recognition in PH
(De Haan et al., 1987; Young et al., 1988)

Background information
PH was a prosopagnosic patient who had sustained a closed head injury as a result of a motorcycle accident. This left him with a broad range of physical and cognitive deficits. Here we focus only on his problems of person identification. He was quite unable to recognize pictures of famous faces overtly, having named only Margaret

---

181

Thatcher's and Ronnie Corbett's faces from any of the hundreds he was tested on. Moreover, when asked to state which of two faces was the famous one, where each pair contained a familiar plus an unfamiliar face, he consistently performed no better than would be expected by chance (e.g. 18 out of 36 correct) (De Haan et al., 1987). In contrast, when asked in a similar task to choose which was the famous person from pairs of names, he performed quite well (e.g. 29 out of 32 correct in De Haan et al.'s 1987 study).

Covert recognition
Although PH appeared quite unable to identify people from their faces overtly, De Haan et al. were able to demonstrate preserved 'covert' recognition of these people in a number of ways. First, they showed that PH was better at deciding that two pictures of a famous face belonged to the same person than two pictures of an unfamiliar face, a finding also observed with normal subjects. Secondly, they showed that when asked to decide upon the occupation of a person from a name, there was interference (PH performed the task more slowly) if the name was accompanied by a picture of a face from a different occupational category compared with conditions where the name appeared alone or accompanied by a face from the same occupational category. So, for example, it would be difficult to judge that the name 'John Wayne' was the name of a film star if it was accompanied by the face of a politician, but less difficult if it was accompanied by the face of another film star. This shows that the faces must, in some sense, be recognized. Again, this mirrored a result obtained with normal subjects. Finally, when asked to learn 'new' names to faces that he could not recognize, PH was better at learning their correct names than incorrect ones. All these findings suggest that PH had subconscious knowledge of the identities of faces that he failed to recognize overtly.

Associative priming
Associative priming can also be used to demonstrate covert recognition. In normal subjects, recognizing a face is speeded if the face is preceded by a face of a closely associated person compared with when it is preceded by an unrelated person (Bruce and Valentine, 1986). Of course, this task could not be tested with PH as he was unable to recognize faces overtly at all. However, Young et al. (1988) demonstrated that PH was faster to decide whether the *names* of people were familiar to him when these were preceded by associatively related faces. Thus, he was faster to decide that Ernie Wise's name was familiar if it immediately followed a picture of the face of Eric Morecambe than if it followed the face of someone quite unrelated, such as Prince Charles. In a post test, it was established that PH could not recognize any of the faces that were used to precede the names in the study, except Margaret Thatcher and Ronnie Corbett, and the associative priming effect occurred even if responses to trials

with these faces were excluded. The facilitation observed from faces to names was no less for PH than was found when normal subjects were tested in an analogous experiment (indeed, the data in Table 3.6 suggest the effect was stronger for PH, though this difference is not significant). Both PH and control subjects were reasonably accurate at the name decision task, though PH generally responded more slowly in the task than did control subjects without brain damage.

Table 3.6 Average reaction times (milliseconds) to decide that names are familiar when preceded by related or unrelated faces (data from Young et al., 1988, Experiments 3 and 4)

	Related	Unrelated	Associative priming effect
PH	1016	1117	101
Controls	627	657	30

The observation that PH matched two pictures of familiar faces better than two pictures of unfamiliar faces demonstrates that he had some preserved knowledge of facial appearances of previously known individuals, but by itself this finding does not establish that he could access identity information. However, the savings in name-learning combined with the interference effects and the associative priming effects which were demonstrated all suggest that PH could access quite specific information about facial identity, and yet he remained quite unable to produce this information overtly.

These observations showing covert recognition prove extremely difficult for the Bruce and Young model to explain. According to the Bruce and Young (1986) model, familiarity judgements were held to be made on the basis of activation levels at the face recognition units, and this formed an early stage in the sequence of establishing the full identity of a person. Given PH's consistent *failure* to make familiarity judgements at better than chance levels, according to this model he should not be able to access information from 'deeper' levels in the system. As will be seen in Section 5.3, however, a slightly different conceptualization of the stages of person identification has helped us to understand these seemingly paradoxical observations.

Summary of Section 5.2

- The Bruce and Young model proposed independent routes for the processing of expressions, facial speech and identities, and a sequence of stages within the identification route.

- The sequence of stages proposed for identification stood up to an attempt at falsification.
- The phenomenon of covert recognition in prosopagnosia suggests that the stage model of identification offered by Bruce and Young requires modification.

5.3   Computer models of person identification

Although the Bruce and Young (1986) model appears to run into difficulties in accounting for some specific phenomena such as covert recognition, a recent **connectionist** implementation of this model (Burton et al., 1990) has allowed an account to be provided of this and other effects. Their artificial intelligence model provides an implementation of the central 'zone' of the Bruce and Young (1986) model: the stages from the recognition of face patterns by the FRUs through to the retrieval of semantic information about personal identity from the PINs. Here we describe the properties of the implemented model in quite general terms. However, all the effects described are based upon detailed simulation experiments using networks considerably more complex than that illustrated. The reader is referred to the original papers for details of the simulations.

To produce a working implementation of these parts of the original model, Burton et al. (1990) were forced to make explicit the relationship between the person identity nodes in the Bruce and Young model and the semantic information which they were held to access. In the Burton et al. implementation, the person identity nodes (PINs) were presented as identity-specific nodes like the nodes for Diana, Charles and Thatcher shown in Figure 3.8, rather than information stores. The PINs receive inputs from recognition systems specialized for faces (FRUs), as well as from other systems specialized for the recognition of written or spoken names (the **name input units**), or voices. These PINs then *access* a further pool of **semantic information units** specifying such things as nationality, occupation, leisure pursuits, and so forth (see Figure 3.8). Once this relationship between the PINs and semantic information has been made explicit, it becomes possible to suggest that the PINs, *not* the FRUs, are the locus at which the decision is taken about whether or not a person is familiar. The PINs provide a common stage at which information is pooled from faces, voices, and other contextual sources, and it seems reasonable to suggest that familiarity should be assessed at the level at which all these information sources combine, rather than isolating a decision about familiarity separately within each of the specific recognition unit systems. In this way, the model implements the earlier suggestion of Young et al. (1985, see

Section 5.1) that the FRUs signalled the degree of resemblance between the face input and the stored representation of face appearance. This resemblance signal is then passed to a later stage (the PINs) at which the information from the FRUs is combined with that from other sources.

The architecture which was chosen to implement this model was an interactive activation and competition connectionist architecture (**IAC model**), which had previously been applied by McClelland, Grossberg and others to a number of problems in cognitive science. The precise architecture used most closely resembles the now well-known 'Jets and Sharks' model of McClelland (1981). Applied to person identification, the IAC model is organized as follows. There are several pools of units, and linked units in different pools are connected by excitatory links as shown by the arrows in Figure 3.8. These links are bi-directional. Thus, the FRU for Prince Charles's face excites the PIN for Prince Charles

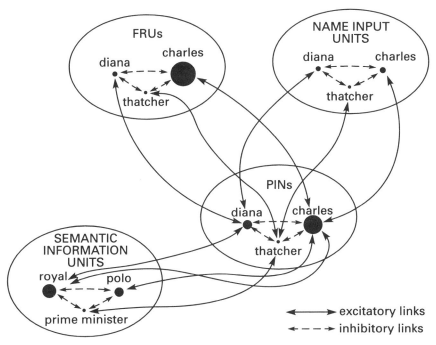

Figure 3.8   The central architecture of Burton et al.'s (1990) IAC model of person identification, showing face and name inputs. The figure illustrates just three units within each of the pools of face recognition units (FRUs), name input units, person identity nodes (PINs), and semantic information units. The size of the units represents how active they are, and the figure illustrates (approximately) the activation that would be expected at each unit during presentation of the face of Prince Charles. Inhibitory links are shown with dashed lines

which in turn excites semantic information units for 'royal', 'architecture', 'polo' and so forth. Excitation also runs in the opposite direction: from 'royal' to Charles's PIN, to Charles's FRU. *Within* each pool, however, all units *inhibit* each other as shown by the dotted arrows. Thus, there is a competition whereby excitement in the FRU for Prince Charles will inhibit activity in other FRUs; the PIN for Prince Charles will inhibit activity in other PINs; and the semantic unit for 'royal' will inhibit activity in other semantic units. This within-pool inhibition means that there is a tendency for just one unit within each pool to become the most active one following the presentation of a hypothetical face. However, because of excitatory connections running in each direction *between* different pools, units which are associated to the same unit in a different pool can nevertheless activate each other. Thus, because the Charles PIN excites the semantic unit 'royal', excitatory links between the 'royal' semantic unit and other PINs, such as that for Princess Diana, Princess Anne, or the Queen, will mean that activation in each of these PINs will also rise a little when the face or name of Charles is presented.

According to the IAC model, the decision that a person is familiar is made when there is sufficient (i.e. above-threshold) activation at the level of the PIN. These properties of the model provide the following account of the 'associative priming' phenomenon described in Techniques Box U. Suppose that the face of Prince Charles is recognized. The activation at the PIN leads to activation of associated semantic information units, and these in turn activate other PINs to which they are linked (e.g. Diana). Despite the fact that inhibition within the PIN system is driving the activation of other PINs down, the shared semantic information will lead to increased activation of associated PINs, offsetting the inhibition they receive from within the PIN system. This means that the PIN corresponding to someone closely associated with Charles, such as Princess Diana (despite their separation!), will also become active: the Prince Charles PIN will activate the 'royal' semantic information unit, and the 'royal' semantic information unit will also activate the Princess Diana PIN. If the face of Princess Diana must be recognized immediately after that of Charles, it will take less activation for Diana's face to produce some criterion level of activation at the PIN, because of the boost to activation received through recognition of her 'partner'. This model thus provides an account of associative priming. Furthermore, according to this model, it does not matter whether the boost to activation at the PIN level has arisen through activation from the face or the name. Faces should be primed by names as well as faces, and this is as observed (see Techniques Box U).

The IAC model can also produce the phenomenon of covert recognition that posed difficulties for the Bruce and Young (1986) model.

Burton et al. (1991) suggested that the behaviour of a patient such as PH might arise if intact face recognition units had only weak connections to the rest of the person identification system. To simulate this, they reduced the connection strengths between intact face recognition units and PINs in the IAC model, so that activation from the FRUs could not produce above-threshold activation at the PINs. In this way, the system models a patient who cannot state that a known face is familiar. The sub-threshold activation at the PINs nevertheless produced sufficient activation in related PINs, via their shared semantic units, to generate an associative priming effect just as great as that obtained in an 'undamaged' network. As indicated in Table 3.6 (see Techniques Box U), the priming effect found in patient PH was at least as big as that found in control subjects. This demonstration therefore provides a possible model of the dissociation between impaired judgement of familiarity and the intact subconscious processing of information about identity which was observed in the patient PH. On this account, the face recognition units do not send strong enough signals to trigger overt recognition of familiar faces, but the weak signals are sufficient to activate information about identity that can be detected covertly.

The IAC model has generated new experimental predictions. One of these concerns the patient ME, described in Section 5.1. Recall that this patient was able to say that faces were familiar, but generally unable to retrieve any specific information about why each person seemed familiar. The patient had the same difficulty when presented with names of people, which she could correctly judge as familiar, without being able to say why. On the IAC model, it would appear that the patient can get no further than the stage of person identity nodes, from which familiarity is signalled. Access to the semantic information system has been lost. Now this account makes the rather counterintuitive prediction that, because the PINs can be accessed from both faces and names, the patient should be able correctly to pair up names with faces, *despite* knowing nothing about them. This prediction was tested by De Haan et al. (1991), who found that ME was indeed able match 23 out of 26 faces with their correct names chosen in each case from a set of three containing one other associated name.

The IAC model has therefore shown that a system of the Bruce and Young type can be implemented in a way which provides an account of observations that the original model found troublesome. In addition to its account of associative priming, and covert recognition, the IAC model was also able to simulate other experimental findings from the face recognition literature. Moreover, like Bruce and Young's model before it, the IAC model makes predictions, and these may be tested through further experimental and neuropsychological investigations.

The results of such investigations may lead to support, or further modification of the model, just as the phenomenon of covert recognition forced the development of the Bruce and Young model into the IAC one.

The IAC model has already been extended beyond what is described here, to provide an account of face distinctiveness effects (Burton et al., 1990) and an account of why names are difficult to retrieve, though this aspect of the model is controversial at present (see Burton and Bruce, 1992, 1993). It has therefore provided a successful and expandable cognitive model of the key stages of person identification. However, whatever its success as a cognitive model, one major deficiency of the IAC model is that it lacks a perceptual 'front end', which can deliver descriptions of real rather than hypothetical face images to match those stored in the FRUs. Future research in this area will be aimed at building links between the representational processes described in Section 3 and the identification processes discussed in this section. A further deficiency of all the models we have described in this section is that they are models of the steady state of the system, and do not provide any account of the processes which allow new face patterns to be learned and new identities to be stored in memory. It will be interesting to see whether the models can be developed in the future to account for how we learn new identities.

Summary of Section 5.3

- Portions of the Bruce and Young model have been implemented using an interactive activation and competition (IAC) architecture.
- In the IAC model, familiarity decisions are taken at the PINs on the basis of activation received from input recognition units for faces, names, voices, etc. PINs access semantic information about personal identity.
- The IAC model has properties which produce associative priming, and which can account for 'covert' recognition.

6   Conclusions: is face recognition a 'special' process?

Part III has introduced face recognition as an example of discrimination within a 'basic level' category of object, and contrasted the representational process with that used in the recognition of other objects (see Section 3.4). A further difference between perceiving faces and other objects is that faces are involved in a number of different social processes, with identification of the person from their face being only one of the many roles played by faces in social interaction. At the perceptual level, then, face processing appears to differ in a number of ways from the processing of other kinds of objects.

At the more cognitive level, however, there are many similarities between the organization of the processes leading to person identification and those involved in the identification of other kinds of objects. For example, associative priming is found in object and word recognition as well as in face recognition (e.g. see Humphreys and Bruce, 1989). Furthermore, it has been pointed out that other 'expert' recognition tasks, such as the identification of dogs by breeders, may show similarities to face processing, even at the perceptual level.

Thus, there are both contrasts and similarities between the findings and theories provided for face recognition and for recognition of other kinds of material. Faces are such important biological stimuli, however, it is possible that they are processed in a manner quite unlike that used for other types of object. If this were so, then this would limit the relevance of studies of face processing for our understanding of object perception and recognition. This last section will examine this possibility.

Hay and Young (1982) distinguished between two senses in which face processing might be 'special':

1 *The dedicated processes hypothesis:* There might be processes specifically dedicated to faces, within a region or regions of cortex not concerned with processing other objects. The processes themselves might be similar to those used in the perception of other object types. On this account, processes occurring within the face-processing area, or module, would be duplicated in other special-purpose modules dealing with other kinds of material, and by studying face processing we could learn about general principles of visual recognition which apply to other kinds of material.

2 *The unique processes hypothesis:* Face perception and recognition might involve *unique* processes, quite unlike those used in the perception of any other kinds of thing.

189

This concluding section will consider briefly whether there is any evidence that face processing involves unique processes.

One piece of evidence which is often used to suggest that faces are 'special', in the sense of unique, is their privileged status in the neonate. Newborn babies only minutes old will follow (with eye and head movements) a schematic face further than a similar but non-face pattern (a scrambled or upside-down arrangement of the same features). Thus, babies must come into the world knowing something about faces as an important and distinct class of objects. However, on the basis of painstaking research and analogies with the process of imprinting in chicks, Johnson and Morton (1991) argue that what is innate is the ability to *pay attention* to faces. The innate attentional bias then acts to direct a different neural system to *learn* about the individual characteristics of faces. There is thus no suggestion that face identification *per se* has an innate head start (pun intended), except that an infant will be more likely to look at face-like things in the first few days of its life. On this account, then, face processing may have a special status in the neonate, just as sucking does, but these early processing systems are superseded by others which may be based on quite different, and quite general, procedures.

Other demonstrations of neonatal proficiency with faces suggest that there may be some innate appreciation of facial gestures and expressions, since there are reports that infants can imitate these (Meltzoff and Moore, 1977). However, we have already argued that the representational demands of expression analysis are much simpler than those of face identification, so it might be that information about expressions is 'hard-wired' in a way that is neither possible, nor sensible, for identities. We have also seen that expression analysis proceeds via an independent processing route in the adult, which would be quite consistent with it having a different developmental status from that of identification.

The observed specialization of cells for faces within the monkey temporal lobe (see Section 4.2) is consistent with the dedicated processes hypothesis, but does not indicate that face processing is unique. Although similar specialization within the monkey brain has not been found for many other objects, cells have also been found which respond selectively to hands (Gross et al., 1969). This suggests that faces are not the only objects to which special regions may be dedicated.

Neuropsychological evidence has sometimes been used to claim a special status for faces, since in some patients face identification seems to be specifically affected by brain damage. However, such observations are generally consistent with dedicated processing rather than uniqueness of face processing. Furthermore, it is rare for prosopagnosic patients to have no problems other than their difficulties with face recognition. Often they are impaired at other visuo-spatial tasks, or other within-category discriminations. Prosopagnosic patients are sometimes, though not always, unable to recognize other classes of objects altogether. Very occasionally there have been reports of patients who have problems recognizing objects but *not* faces (see Ellis and Young, 1989). This is problematic for an account in which within-category differentiation is *contingent upon* some more basic level of object classification, but is not problematic for an account (as developed in this part) which states that there may be processes specifically dedicated to differentiating faces, which operate independently of those required to identify basic level objects.

The detailed pattern of association and dissociation between face recognition and recognition of other objects, whether at basic level or within category, is actually quite bewildering, and on balance contributes rather little to debates about dedicated processes versus uniqueness. As an example, consider the dissociations that have been reported in the literature between recognition of faces and animals. For some reason, prosopagnosia seems to be an occupational hazard for farmers, or people with interests in farm animals. There has been a report of a prosopagnosic farmer who remains able to identify his cows (Bruyer et al., 1983), but another whose ability to recognize faces improved but who remained unable to identify cows (Assal et al., 1984), and a more recent case of a prosopagnosic patient who took up sheep farming after his injury, and developed extraordinary expertise at sheep recognition (McNeill and Warrington, 1993). Such observations contribute little to the debate about uniqueness. However, the fact that quite discrete abilities of these kinds can be selectively impaired or preserved does lend some support to the notion that there are face-*specific* processing areas in the brain, as there may perhaps be other areas specific for other kinds of object (Ellis and Young, 1989).

To sum up, evidence from physiology and neuropsychology is consistent with there being face-specific brain areas or processing modules, but does not suggest that face identification is special in the stronger sense of 'uniqueness'. Evidence from neonatal face perception suggests that there may be some inborn mechanisms for attending to, but not for learning, faces, and perhaps also for recognizing and responding to facial expressions. It may be that expression perception and production involve processing mechanisms quite unique to faces, but as this route is independent of that used for face identification, it leaves open the possibility that the identification of faces duplicates the information-processing mechanisms used with other kinds of material.

Indeed, at a deeper level in the cognitive system, there is reasonably strong evidence that the organization of the different 'modules' involved in face identification is very similar to that implicated in the recognition of other aspects of person identification (e.g. voice recognition), and to that used for object recognition more generally. Bruce and Young (1986) described how basic effects, such as those of associative priming, appeared to be similar for face recognition and for object recognition. At the level of individual identification there are similarities too. Brennen et al. (1990) (see Techniques Box T) found results in tip-of-the-tongue experiments requiring the identification of famous buildings which were similar to those found with identification of famous people. Johnston and Bruce (1994) showed that the identification of cartoon characters such as Mickey Mouse showed the same patterns of associative priming as those observed in face recognition. In short, it seems that the account developed in Section 5 for face recognition is not at all idiosyncratic. While there may be processing routes *specific* to face recognition, their organization would appear to be similar to those used for a range of other materials. If there are 'unique' aspects of face perception, these seem more likely to lie in the processing of facial expressions and speech where it is difficult, or impossible, to find parallel skills relating to other objects.

Summary of Section 6

- Evidence relevant to the issue of whether face processing is 'special' is obtained from developmental, neuropsychological and neurophysiological sources.
- There is some evidence for processes specifically dedicated to faces, but rather little evidence to suggest that faces are processed by 'unique' mechanisms.

Coda

The past ten years have seen considerable progress in our understanding of the perceptual and cognitive processes involved in deriving meaning from faces. One reason for the relatively rapid progress has been the use of increasingly sophisticated computer graphics and modelling techniques, which have allowed images to be created, and ideas to be tested, in novel ways. A further reason is that faces are natural, biological images that are intrinsically interesting to scientists wishing to move towards increasing the ecological validity of their research. A final reason is the range of applications which should benefit from our increased understanding of human face processing. Progress in this field is sufficiently rapid that an account such as this could not have been written ten years ago, and in only a few years time we should have several further pieces of the puzzle in place. It is hoped that this material will motivate students to follow up for themselves the further advances in this rapidly developing field.

Further reading

BRUCE, V. (1988) *Recognising Faces*, Lawrence Erlbaum Associates.

BRUCE, V., COWEY, A., ELLIS, A.W. and PERRETT, D.I. (eds) (1992) *Processing the Facial Image: Proceedings of a Royal Society Discussion Meeting*, Oxford University Press.

YOUNG, A.W. and ELLIS, H.D. (eds) (1989) *Handbook of Research on Face Processing*, North Holland.

Overview

Ilona Roth

The common theme running throughout this book has been an exploration of the perceptual and cognitive processes by which we make sense of the world around us, and in particular some of its most significant entities: objects and people.

Underlying our ability to make sense of the world are the related processes of categorization and recognition. When we recognize an object, it normally follows that we know what the object is for (or, in the case of a living object, how it will behave) and what it is called. Similarly, recognizing someone's face normally evokes knowledge about the person (friend, bank manager, member of the royal family) and what their name is. Most of the exceptions to these consequences of recognition occur when people have sustained brain injury. The resulting dissociations mean that, in a very real way, these unfortunate people cannot make full sense of their world. The man who could make gestures appropriate to an object's function but could not name it, or the woman who could recognize facial expressions of emotion but not the people who made them, have both been deprived of important aspects of their grasp on reality.

Parts I, II and III covered, respectively, the topics of assigning objects to appropriate mental categories, recognizing the category membership of objects from their visual appearance, and of identifying specific objects (in this case faces) within a category. These achievements impose the conflicting cognitive requirements of generalizing across individually different objects and of discriminating between them. All three parts of the book made the intuitively plausible assumption that complex representations and processes are necessary to meet these requirements. Here, let us consider what these representations and processes are.

Representations

> A representation is something that stands for something else. In other words, it is a kind of model of the thing it represents. We have to distinguish between a *representing world* and a *represented world*. The representing world must somehow mirror some aspects of the represented world. (Rumelhart and Norman, 1985, p.16)

In the theories discussed in this book, the represented world is the physical world of patterns and objects, animals, plants, and human faces. Of course, many of the theories have dealt with very limited or simplified aspects of this exceedingly complex world. For instance, experimental studies usually employ two-dimensional pictures rather than three-dimensional objects. AI models such as Marr's may be able to cope with three-dimensional objects, but only a small repertoire of such objects is actually recognized.

Three main classes of 'representing worlds' have been considered throughout the book:

1 Relatively enduring representations stored in long-term memory.
2 Relatively temporary representations which are constructed as intermediate stages in the processing of sensory input.
3 New representations which are the 'final product' of perceptual processing.

In many ways this is an artificial division, because perception involves a continuous cycle of interaction between all three types of representation. For instance, an object may be recognized as a table, while simultaneously furnishing novel features (three legs rather than four) which serve to update the perceiver's stored knowledge of typical tables. A person may be recognized as a familiar friend — Jane Smith — while at the same time providing the perceiver with new information about her, such as a change of hairstyle. Dividing this cycle into different types of representation is simply convenient for purposes of discussion.

1 Representations stored in long-term memory
Part I dealt with several different views of enduring representations. Traditionally, representations for categories such as chair, table, dog, or rose were assumed to consist of lists of features which would define these categories. It was Eleanor Rosch who highlighted the difficulties of defining everyday categories and established the importance of fuzzy representations, proposing initially that everyday categories are represented by single composite prototypes based on typical instances. There were two reformulations of this idea: one assumed that categories are represented by a summary list of typical features, the other assumed that category representations consist of specific, typical exemplars.

Rosch also stressed the importance of hierarchical relationships in representing conceptual information, arguing that one level in such hierarchies (the basic level) would have special properties as a representation. For most purposes, the basic level is the most economical level for cognitive activity: this level takes priority for categorization and visual recognition of objects. For face recognition, however, the principle focus of activity is *below* this basic level: face recognition represents a highly developed ability to differentiate between 'objects' (i.e. faces) which fall within the same basic level category. We are natural experts at recognizing faces, but expertise in other areas may also bring about shifts in the primary focus of categorization: the basic categorizations of plants made by Tzeltal Indians were more specific (more 'expert') than those made by westerners. Similarly specific distinctions were made by dog experts.

Like many theoretical dichotomies, the notion that well-defined and fuzzy representations are mutually exclusive alternatives has inevitably come under attack. Part I introduced the more recent 'dual representation view', according to which many concepts lend themselves to both well-defined and fuzzy types of representation. An important conclusion was that the *purpose* of categorization is a critical factor in how categories are represented. Category representations may vary depending on whether they are for everyday or expert use, whether they are formed to meet specific goals or to represent the state of the world as we know it.

Part II considered what kinds of stored representations are required for visual object recognition. The general framework underpinning this discussion was that of structural descriptions. This represents a development of the feature models discussed in Part I in emphasizing the importance of *relations* among features: it is not just that a table has four legs and a flat top but how these components are related which is crucial for visual recognition. Both Marr and Nishihara's generalized cylinders and Biederman's geons are attempts to specify just what type of stored structural descriptions would provide a basis for recognition.

Part III also postulated stored structural descriptions, this time in the form of 'face recognition units' as the basis for our ability to recognize a face from its visual appearance. But notice that Part III added a further refinement to this structural description approach. It was argued that, whereas components (features, geons, etc.) and their structural relations provide an adequate basis for recognizing visually presented objects, for face recognition, *interactions* among these components may be important. The implication is that the stored descriptions for recognizing faces take the form of complex configurations of the components, or even holistic descriptions in which the components are not made explicit. Common to both Part II and Part III is the idea that the basic structural information, whether about objects or faces, is stored separately from semantic and name information.

2 Temporary representations of input

Part I of this book has little to say abut the relatively transient representations which are thought to mediate perceptual recognition. In contrast, Part II considers these representations in some detail, following in outline the account offered by David Marr. Thus, the grey level description, raw primal sketch and full primal sketch can all be thought of as transient representations, each of which makes explicit certain aspects of the input relevant to the recognition process. Even structural descriptions can be thought of as temporary representations derived from input, as well as being permanent members of a stored catalogue with which this input is compared.

Notice that not all dimensions of input are represented in Marr's representational stages: instead, these take the form of fairly *selective* assertions about those properties of input relevant to object recognition. In Marr's model, and to a large extent in Biederman's, information about the edges and main internal contours of objects is preserved at the expense of surface characteristics such as colour or texture. The successful implementations of Marr's model, and the supportive experimental evidence for Biederman's, both suggest that outline information *is* of paramount importance in recognizing objects. By contrast, Part III provides convincing evidence that surface characteristics such as pigmentation and shading are as important as outline in identifying faces. It follows that these surface characteristics must be included in the intermediate representations mediating face recognition. This may require a different account of the primal sketch from Marr's: perhaps one like Watt's model in which information about actual intensity levels in the image, rather than just intensity changes, is preserved.

In Part II, one of the overriding roles outlined for the 'transient' stages in processing input is to convert the initial viewpoint centred descriptions into object-centred descriptions which are invariant across viewpoints. Biederman's model offered an elegant solution to this, in which certain geon characteristics are themselves invariant across viewpoints. The same need for invariance applies equally to face recognition, since we must be able to recognize a face despite changes in viewing angle, lighting and so on. Yet, it seems that this might be done by storing representations from multiple viewpoints, rather than a single viewpoint independent representation.

3 New representations of input

New representations which are formed as a result of processing input are, in many ways, the most complex and elusive for psychologists to describe. If we make a conscious effort to introspect, we can examine the contents of our awareness, which encompasses inanimate objects, animate creatures and, above all, human beings. Familiar though these experiences are in some respects, they are constantly changing too. We may never view an object twice from the same angle or in the same lighting conditions. We may encounter new objects which we none the less recognize as members of familiar categories, or meet new people who soon become 'recognizable' as stored knowledge is updated. What are the mental representations which correspond to this moment-to-moment, constantly updating awareness?

Most of the theories discussed in this book tackle this question only indirectly by specifying outputs of the kind which can be measured or described. These include subjective reports of how two-dimensional patterns look (Part II); reaction times to assign words to categories or to name pictured objects (Parts I and II); errors in naming pictured objects or faces, particularly by neuropsychological patients (Parts II and III); computer printouts describing what objects are present in a scene (Part II), and both computer outputs and human responses indicating whether a face is familiar (Part III). Most of us probably share the feeling that none of these outputs constitutes the *real* essence of perceptual experience: that our awareness constitutes something beyond this. But it is equally mistaken to imagine that this 'extra' quality takes the form of discrete 'mental objects', similar to pictures in the mind. Recognizing that an object is a table is certainly not the same as experiencing a mental picture of it, or even having its name 'pop' into one's mind. It does, however, seem to be intimately connected with the ability to plan what one can do with the object, how to walk round it without collision, and so on.

There is much research to be done in this area. While many believe that this lies only in the realm of philosophy, scientists such as Crick (1994) believe that awareness itself will eventually yield its secrets through the methods of neuroscience and psychology.

Processes

Another important theme of this volume concerns the processes by which inputs are transformed into representations resulting in categorization, recognition and identification. Again, though, the distinction between representations and processes is a matter of convenience rather than clear definition.

The models discussed in Part I made few explicit references to processes. However, all made the general assumption that items are assigned to categories by comparison and matching with stored representations. Processes were more to the fore in Part II, with the assumption, drawn from Marr's model, of an essentially sequential transformation of input through a series of increasingly complex modules, culminating in a matching process at recognition. Marr's rationale for this 'bottom-up' mode of explanation is that the information in the retinal image is sufficiently 'rich' to provide the basis for object recognition without the logically tricky notion of top-down hypotheses which guide interpretation of 'what's there'. While processing in Marr's model proceeds to a high level without using specific object knowledge, it *is* guided by general rules, embodied in the vision system, about the way the world is organized (e.g. adjacent regions in the input are likely to belong to the same object; an object cannot be in two places at once). One could certainly argue that these general rules constitute a kind of stored knowledge, albeit less specific than the object hypotheses assumed by 'top-down' models. And, as we saw, even Marr's program employs some top-down knowledge: in the first place to resolve those ambiguities which cannot be resolved bottom-up, and in the second place to draw final conclusions about the identity of objects.

Marr's model implied more than just a unidirectional flow of information: it assumed that the modules which process this flow operate independently and sequentially. Evidence presented towards the end of Part II suggested a rather different conceptualization, known as a cascade model, in which information is continuously 'fed forward' through the stages of the system, rather than being processed through one discrete stage at a time.

Part III also raised questions about the dependence or independence of processing modules. There seems to be clear evidence that facial speech and facial expressions are processed separately from information about facial appearance. The model initially proposed by Bruce and Young suggested processing modules which operate independently but *in parallel* to one another.

Both the cascade model in Part II and the Bruce and Young model in Part III represent attempts to address what are clearly complex patterns of both interaction and independence among processing stages. It is but a short step from these to the contemporary generation of connectionist models which seek to model the recognition process in a highly interactive network of excitatory and inhibitory connections, not unlike those in a real nervous system. Just one example of this approach is provided by the IAC model in Part III.

Levels of explanation

A third theme of this volume has been an exploration of the different but complementary methods used in investigating how we categorize concepts and recognize objects and people. Part II introduced Marr's claim that three different levels of analysis, computational, algorithmic and hardware, contribute to this endeavour. As we saw, different research methods do not all generate insights at the same levels.

Marr's own view was that the computational theory level took precedence over the other two levels. He argued that any real insight into perception must commence with a formal analysis of the task which is accomplished in perception: a computational theory which, by implication, lies within the realm of artificial intelligence. Because, according to Marr, it is in principle possible for this computational task to be accomplished using a variety of algorithms and 'hardware', he saw these latter levels of analysis as subsidiary. His view was that methods such as neurophysiology, neuropsychology and human experimentation, which tell us about the processing algorithms of natural vision and about the underlying 'hardware', provide lesser insights that the methods of artificial intelligence.

The equal weighting given in this book to the different methods discussed testifies to the fact that views about explanation have moved on from Marr. A variety of computer algorithms and electronic hardware may in principle implement the same computational theory in an artificial vision system; but in natural vision systems, the algorithms and hardware take specific forms which appear to impose constraints on what perceptual 'computations' can be accomplished. It is therefore appropriate to 'set the agenda' as much by the insights provided by neurophysiology, neuropsychology and human experimentation as by the insights from artificial intelligence. The most recent generation of artificial intelligence models, as exemplified by the connectionist IAC model discussed in Part III, are directly informed by the network-type hardware assumed to operate in biological systems. None the less, Marr's general point, that we must not lose sight of the overall 'nature of the task' represented by our capacity to see and recognize objects and people, remains important.

Answers to SAQs

SAQ 1

(a) The list of properties is not sufficient for the category 'square' because it applies not only to squares but to other four-sided figures such as rectangles and parallelograms. Thus, a figure which possesses this list of properties is not guaranteed to be a member of the category 'square'.

(b) If we add the properties 'All sides are equal' and 'All angles are 90°' the description becomes necessary and sufficient for the category 'square' (i.e. any figure possessing the properties is guaranteed to be a square).

SAQ 2

Taking the group of assumptions on page 24, the fact that subjects appear to verify statements about some category members (e.g. 'robin') faster than others (e.g. 'parrot') suggests, in contrast to the defining feature approach, that the category representation does not apply equally to both these category members: the two members have a different status within the category. This implies, in turn, that the representation of the category does *not* take the form of a definition comprising necessary and sufficient properties: this form of representation would apply equally to all category members.

Collins and Quillian's findings do not bear directly on whether all concepts are represented by lists of defining features: they only investigated biological concepts.

The fact that, contrary to the predictions of Collins and Quillian's model, subjects took longer to search for 'a dog is a mammal' than 'a dog is an animal' suggests a discrepancy between their mentally represented hierarchy for animals and the zoologically based hierarchy assumed by Collins and Quillian. The defining feature approach does not easily accommodate such individual variations in mental representation.

Taking the assumption on page 26, Collins and Quillian's pattern of results is broadly in keeping with the claim that people organize concepts hierarchically, but a strict pattern of property inheritance cannot be assumed in all cases. Even within their model, special properties had to be devised (e.g. ostriches cannot fly) which are contrary to the strict pattern of inheritance suggested by the model.

SAQ 3

(a) and (b) are properties which an object must have to be a chair.

SAQ 4

As we have seen, only two of the six properties in the list, (a) and (b), are necessary properties. The others are all properties which chairs usually have, but an object can be a chair without having them. None of the properties on the list is sufficient for chairs because they also apply to other items of furniture such as seats, benches and sofas.

Answers to SAQs

SAQ 5
Here are the category items arranged in order of the mean typicality rating given to them by Rosch's subjects:

Category item	Mean typicality rating
Pea	1.07
Sweetcorn	1.55
Lettuce	1.85
Artichoke	2.32
Radish	2.51
Parsnip	2.91
Leek	3.15
Mushroom	3.56
Pumpkin	4.74
Rice	5.59

As you can see, Rosch's subjects rated pea as a highly typical category member and rice as a pretty atypical category member, with the other items occupying a range of values in between. Your own typicality ratings, which are not based on means, will be in whole numbers, but you can still look at whether the numerical ratings are similar, and whether the rank order of items is the same.

One reason for any differences between your ratings and those of Rosch's subjects may be the different dietary habits of the British and American cultures. For instance, 'sweetcorn' is a very widely used vegetable in the USA, and probably less widely used in this country, so we might expect Americans to give it a higher typicality rating.

SAQ 6
According to the typicality ratings given in Table 1.2, chair is more typical than clock and so should be categorized faster. From the typicality ratings given in the answer to SAQ 5, radish is more typical than mushroom, so should be categorized faster.

SAQ 7
(a) The relative cue validity for the three features is:
    Feathers   (Most)
    Flies
    Brown colour   (Least)
    'Feathers' would be the most useful feature in deciding whether an entity was a bird because it is usually associated with birds and rarely associated with other concepts. 'Brown colour' would be the least useful because, although quite a few birds are brown, so are many other animals and other objects: similarly, there are quite a few birds which are *not* brown. 'Flying' is quite distinctive, but it is also a feature of insects and aeroplanes, as well as some mammals, angels, etc.!

(b) Each of the birds has two of the three features on the above list. But 'parrot' has the more highly weighted combination of features ('feathers' and 'flies'), whereas 'emu' has the less highly weighted combination ('feathers' and 'brown colour'). 'Parrot' should therefore be a more typical exemplar of the concept 'bird'.

SAQ 8
Remember that, in 'limited' exemplar models, the stored representation consists of typical exemplars that the person has encountered. A new instance which is fairly atypical may bear little resemblance to any of the stored exemplars, and may in fact resemble the stored exemplars of other concepts. A contextual cue (e.g. 'Imagine the object on a shelf with flowers in it') may serve to bias a person's decision about which category the object actually belongs to.

SAQ 9
According to Berlin's findings, the intermediate level should be basic for the bird hierarchy. For the furniture hierarchy, intermediate categories such as 'chair' intuitively seem more distinctive and coherent.

SAQ 10
The location of the basic level may vary between individuals or between groups depending on demands of their culture and the amount of knowledge they have. It seems that, for the average westerner, the distinctive biological groupings are at the level of 'tree', 'bird', 'fish', etc. Other cultural groups, such as the Tzeltal Indians, may require more sophisticated knowledge in order, for example, to construct dwellings from one type of tree rather than another. So, for them, it is the more specific intermediate categories which are basic. Of course the basic level may shift — as when a western person acquires expert knowledge about birds, trees, etc.

SAQ 11
Reading. Children have to be taught to recognize letter shapes, to associate these with sounds, and to interpret patterns of letter shapes as words. These are clearly effortful processes. In most adults, these processes occur without effort, and are automatic, as illustrated by the fact that we take in information from noticeboards, advertisements, even without intending to.

SAQ 12
Neuropsychology is mainly informative at Marr's levels two and three: it sheds light on the organization of processes and representations responsible for object recognition, and on the underlying brain mechanisms.

SAQ 13
The highest intensity points are represented by any pixel with the value 38, the lowest by any pixel with the value 1.

SAQ 14

Large changes in intensity are indicated with arrows in the figure shown opposite.

Working from left to right, there is a large drop in the intensity of reflected light at the edge between the background and the silhouette of the Mona Lisa. There is a moderate rise at the edge between the hairline and the face, followed by a drop at the outer corner of the eye. There is a large rise where the shadow in the corner of the eye becomes the white of the eye, and a drop again at the edge between the white and the pupil. There is a very large (but broken) rise defining one side of the nose bridge, matched at the other side of the nose bridge by a large drop where a heavy shadow falls. The white of the other eye and its boundary with the pupil are again defined by a large rise and fall. Finally, a large rise and fall accompany the shadows formed by the curving profile of the cheekbone. Though some of these are important 'edges', there are other important edges which, because of the angle of lighting, are not picked out in this way (e.g. the right-hand hairline). Some of these large intensity changes also correspond more closely to the boundaries of shadows than to features *per se*. Finally, there are also small scale changes in intensity all the way along the line, which do not coincide with anything significant in the object.

SAQ 15

A square seems the 'best' and 'simplest' organization of the four dots, and therefore conforms to the Law of Prägnanz. Most people should actually report seeing the figure as a square.

SAQ 16

For 'b': vertical line with closed loop attached at the bottom right.
For 'd': vertical line with closed loop attached at the bottom left.
For 'p': vertical line with closed loop attached at the top right.

SAQ 17

Only the third description applies to both line drawings: it is the only description which is object-centred rather than viewer-centred.

SAQ 18

Your description probably came out something like this:

A rectangular block with a type of curved arc attached to the right-hand surface. On top of the block towards the front left-hand corner is a type of funnel with a bend in it. A zig-zag square section pipe runs from the funnel to a wedge, the smaller end of which is attached to the upper surface of the block at its far right-hand corner.

SAQ 19

(a) Rectangular block
     Curved arc (handle)
     Cylinder
(b) Just these three components put together in different ways can yield four different objects. The attaché case and slide drawer share the same two geon components, as do the cup and the bucket.

Answers to SAQs

SAQ 20
Relative size: G1 bigger than G2.
Verticality: G1 to the side of G2.
Centring: G2 centred on G1 at join.
Relative size of surfaces at join: G2 joined to short surface of G1.

SAQ 21
Humphreys et al. had argued that JB's inability to name visually presented objects arose because he could not access semantic information from the structural system, which in turn affected his ability to name them. The fact that JB was able to produce appropriate gestures does not quite fit in because it suggests that on seeing an object he *was* able to access some information relevant to its use. One possibility is that relevant gestures are not stored within the semantic system, but in some separate motor store, accessed directly from vision. The implication in JB's case would be that the brain lesion had not disrupted this access route.

SAQ 22
The face contributes to the *identification* of people, *understanding emotions* via expression analysis, *understanding speech* through lipreading, *control of dialogue* via perception of the direction of gaze, and assessment of *attractiveness*. For identification, and probably for attractiveness too, all face features including the external (hair) and internal features (eyes, nose, mouth) convey information. For expression analysis, only the internal face features contribute. For lipreading, it is the lower face features (mouth and jaws) which convey information, and for gaze it is the eyes and head direction that are important.

SAQ 23
If several face features differ between two faces, the overall configuration differs more than if just one face feature differs, so even a model which proposed that faces were processed more 'holistically' would predict the results obtained by Bradshaw and Wallace (1971). A second possible reason for such results is that the demands of the task may *force* subjects to inspect each feature of the face in turn. Tasks in which subjects make same–different comparisons do not necessarily tell us about the processes which normally allow us to recognize faces.

SAQ 24
In order to recognize a person's identity, from stimuli where two half faces are inappropriately combined, subjects need to be able to treat the features of each face half in isolation. But configural processing of the upright face composites makes it harder to do this. When the faces are turned upside down, subjects do not process the features as a configuration. Thus, it becomes easier to use the isolated features of each half of the composite face for identification.

SAQ 25
To summarize, there are three possible accounts of the illusion, in terms of: (1) impaired processing of expressions in the inverted face; (2) conflicting reference frames in the inverted face; and (3) impaired configural processing of the inverted face. See the text following SAQ 25 for the full answer to this question.

SAQ 26
Negative images of faces may be hard to recognize because:
(a) they are unfamiliar;
(b) the pigmentation values are wrong (light hair and skin appear dark, and vice versa);
(c) the shading patterns are wrong.

SAQ 27
Automatic search or recognition of faces could be useful for:
(a) searching for known terrorists in areas of high security (e.g. airports);
(b) searching images taken by security cameras for occurrences of missing persons or victims of crime;
(c) comparing images taken by security cameras with stored pictures of prior offenders;
(d) verifying personal identity at cash dispensers;
(e) verifying personal identity at entry to workplace.
For applications such as (d) and (e), it should be possible to control image size, lighting, background and viewpoint by constraining the situation where the face is checked. For other applications such as (a) through to (c), such factors cannot be controlled and the chances of an automatic solution that would be more reliable than human vision seem remote.

SAQ 28
The results showing an advantage for identification of distinctive compared with typical faces are the opposite of those found in the basic level categorization of objects, where there is an advantage for typical items compared with distinctive or atypical ones. For example, it is easier to verify that a sparrow is a bird than that an ostrich is a bird. Distinctiveness is an advantage when identifying individuals but typicality is an advantage when assigning individuals to categories.

SAQ 29
Yes. Some patients can recognize expressions but not identities, while others appear to be impaired at recognizing expressions but are not impaired at deciding about occupations of faces, a task which requires access to the level of individual identity.

SAQ 30
If lipreading really does proceed independently of face identification, then the incidence of McGurk effects should *not* be affected by the mismatch of identities. This prediction is currently being tested in ongoing research.

SAQ 31
Seeing a picture of the person should *not* help, but seeing the initials of the missing name *should* help. If the person's identity is known, then the stage of person identity nodes must have been reached, and additional input via the face recognition units should not help. However, if the route to the name is blocked, then providing partial information about the name, from the initials, should help.

References

ARMSTRONG, S.L., GLEITMAN, L.R. and GLEITMAN, H. (1983) 'What some concepts might not be', *Cognition*, 13, pp.263–308.

ASSAL, G., FAVRE, C. and ANDERES, J.P. (1984) 'Non-reconnaissance d'animaux familiers chez un paysan', *Revue Neurologique*, 140, pp.580–4.

BARSALOU, L.W. (1983) 'Ad hoc categories', *Memory and Cognition*, II (3), pp.211–27.

BARSALOU, L.W. (1991) 'Deriving categories to achieve goals' in Bower, G.H. (ed.) *The Psychology of Learning and Motivation: Advances in Research and Theory* (vol.27, pp.1–64), Academic Press.

BARSALOU, L.W. (1992) *Cognitive Psychology: An Overview for Cognitive Scientists*, Lawrence Erlbaum Associates.

BARSALOU, L.W. and SEWELL, D.R. (1984) *Constructing Categories from Different Points of View* (Emory Cognition Report, no.2), Emory University, Atlanta, G.A.

BARTLETT, J.C. and SEARCY, J. (1993) 'Inversion and configuration of faces', *Cognitive Psychology*, 25, pp.281–316.

BAUER, R.M. (1984) 'Autonomic recognition of names and faces in prosopagnosia: a neuropsychological application of the guilty knowledge test', *Neuropsychologia*, 22, pp.457–69.

BENSON, P.J. and PERRETT, D.I. (1991) 'Perception and recognition of photographic quality facial caricatures: implications for the recognition of natural images', *European Journal of Cognitive Psychology*, 3, pp.105–35.

BERLIN, B. (1972) 'Speculations on the growth of ethno-botanical nomenclature', *Language in Society*, 1, pp.51–86.

BIEDERMAN, I. (1987) 'Recognition-by-components: a theory of human image understanding', *Psychological Review*, 94, pp.115–47.

BRADSHAW, J.L. and WALLACE, G. (1971) 'Models for the processing and identification of faces', *Perception and Psychophysics*, 9, pp.443–8.

BRENNEN, T., BAGULEY, T., BRIGHT, J. and BRUCE, V. (1990) 'Resolving semantically induced tip-of-the-tongue states for proper nouns', *Memory and Cognition*, 18, pp.339–47.

BRUCE, V. (1979) 'Searching for politicians: an information-processing approach to face recognition', *Quarterly Journal of Experimental Psychology*, 31, pp.373–95.

BRUCE, V. (1982) 'Changing faces: visual and non-visual coding processes in face recognition', *British Journal of Psychology*, 73, pp.105–16.

BRUCE, V. (1986) 'Influences of familiarity on the processing of faces', *Perception*, 15, pp.387–97.

BRUCE, V. (1988) *Recognising Faces*, Lawrence Erlbaum Associates.

BRUCE, V., BURTON, A.M. and DENCH, N. (1994) 'What's distinctive about a distinctive face?', *Quarterly Journal of Experimental Psychology*, 47A, pp.119–42.

BRUCE, V., COWEY, A., ELLIS, A.W. and PERRETT, D.I. (eds) (1992) *Processing the Facial Image: Proceedings of a Royal Society Discussion Meeting*, Oxford University Press.

References

BRUCE, V. and GREEN, P.R. (1990) *Visual Perception: Physiology, Psychology and Ecology* (2nd edn), Lawrence Erlbaum Associates.

BRUCE, V., HANNA, E., DENCH, N., HEALEY, P. and BURTON, A.M. (1992) 'The importance of "mass" in line-drawings of faces', *Applied Cognitive Psychology*, 6, pp.619–28.

BRUCE, V. and LANGTON, S. (1994) 'The use of pigmentation and shading information in recognising the sex and identities of faces', *Perception*, in press.

BRUCE, V. and VALENTINE, T. (1986) 'Semantic priming of familiar faces', *Quarterly Journal of Experimental Psychology*, 38A, pp.125–50.

BRUCE, V. and YOUNG, A.W. (1986) 'Understanding face recognition', *British Journal of Psychology*, 77, pp.305–27.

BRUYER, R., LATERRE, C., SERON, X., FEYEREISEN, P., STRYPSTEIN, E., PIERRARD, E. and RECTEM, D. (1983) 'A case of prosopagnosia with some preserved remembrance of familiar faces', *Brain and Cognition*, 2, pp. 257–84.

BURTON, A.M. and BRUCE, V. (1992) 'I recognise your face but I can't remember your name: a simple explanation?', *British Journal of Psychology*, 83, pp.45–60.

BURTON, A.M. and BRUCE, V. (1993) 'Naming faces and naming names', *Memory*, 1, pp.457–80.

BURTON, A.M., BRUCE, V. and JOHNSTON, R.A. (1990) 'Understanding face recognition with an interactive activation model', *British Journal of Psychology*, 81, pp.361–80.

BURTON, A.M., YOUNG, A.W., BRUCE, V., JOHNSTON, R.A. and ELLIS, A.W. (1991) 'Understanding covert recognition', *Cognition*, 39, pp.129–66.

CAMPBELL, R., LANDIS, T. and REGARD, M. (1986) 'Face recognition and lipreading: a neurological dissociation', *Brain*, 109, pp.509–21.

CAREY, S. (1981) 'The development of face perception', in Davies, G., Ellis, H.D. and Shepherd, J. (eds) *Perceiving and Remembering Faces*, Academic Press.

CAREY, S. (1992) 'On becoming a face expert', *Philosophical Transactions of the Royal Society of London*, B335, pp.95–103.

COLLINS, A. and QUILLIAN, M.R. (1969) 'Retrieval time from semantic memory', *Journal of Verbal Learning and Verbal Behaviour*, 8, pp.240–7.

CRICK, F. (1994) *The Astonishing Hypothesis: The Scientific Search for the Soul*, Macmillan.

DAVIES, G.M., ELLIS, H.D. and SHEPHERD, J.W. (1978) 'Face recognition accuracy as a function of mode of representation', *Journal of Applied Psychology*, 63, pp.180–7.

DE HAAN, E.H.F., YOUNG, A.W. and NEWCOMBE, F. (1987) 'Face recognition without awareness', *Cognitive Neuropsychology*, 4, pp.385–415.

DE HAAN, E.H.F., YOUNG, A.W. and NEWCOMBE, F. (1991) 'A dissociation between the sense of familiarity and access to semantic information concerning familiar people', *European Journal of Cognitive Psychology*, 3, pp.51–67.

DEVLIN, LORD PATRICK (1976) *Report to the Secretary of State for the Home Department of the Departmental Committee on Evidence of Identification in Criminal Cases*, HMSO.

DIAMOND, R. and CAREY, S. (1986) 'Why faces are and are not special: an effect of expertise', *Journal of Experimental Psychology: General*, 115, pp.107–17.

EKMAN, P. (ed.) (1982) *Emotion and the Human Face* (2nd edn), Cambridge University Press.

ELLIS, H.D. (1986) 'Processes underlying face recognition', in Bruyer, R. (ed.) *The Neuropsychology of Face Perception and Facial Expression*, Lawrence Erlbaum Associates.

ELLIS, H.D. and YOUNG, A.W. (1989) 'Are faces special?', in Young, A.W. and Ellis, H.D. (eds) *Handbook of Research on Face Processing*, North Holland.

EYSENCK, M.W. and KEANE, M. (1990) *Cognitive Psychology: A Student's Handbook*, Lawrence Erlbaum Associates.

FLUDE, B.M., ELLIS, A.W. and KAY, J. (1989) 'Face processing and and retrieval in an anomic aphasia: names are stored separately from semantic information about people', *Brain and Cognition*, 11, pp.60–72.

FRISBY, J.P. (1979) *Seeing: Illusion, Brain and Mind*, Oxford University Press.

GALPER, R.E. and HOCHBERG, J. (1971) 'Recognition memory for photographs of faces', *American Journal of Psychology*, 84, pp.351–4.

GREEN, K.P., KUHL, P.K., MELTZOFF, A.N. and STEVENS, E.B. (1991) 'Integrating speech information across talkers, gender, and sensory modality: female faces and male voices in the McGurk effect', *Perception and Psychophysics*, 50, pp.524–36.

GROSS, C. (1992) 'Representation of visual stimuli in inferior temporal cortex', *Philosophical Transactions of the Royal Society of London*, B335, pp.3–10.

GROSS, C.G., BENDER, D.B., and ROCHA-MIRANDA, C.E. (1969) 'Visual receptive fields of neurons in inferotemporal cortex of the monkey', *Science*, 166, pp.1303–6.

HANLEY, J.R. and COWELL, E.S. (1988) 'The effects of different types of retrieval cue on the recall of names of famous faces', *Memory and Cognition*, 16, pp.545–55.

HASSELMO, M.E., ROLLS, E.T. and BAYLIS, G.C. (1989) 'The role of expression and identity in the face-selective responses of neurons in the temporal visual cortex of the monkey', *Behavioural Brain Research*, 32, pp.203–18.

HAY, D.C. and YOUNG, A.W. (1982) 'The human face', in Ellis, A.W. (ed.) *Normality and Pathology in Cognitive Functions*, Academic Press.

HAYES, T., MORRONE, M.C. and BURR, D.C. (1986) 'Recognition of positive and negative bandpass-filtered images', *Perception*, 15, pp.595–602.

HEYWOOD, C.A. and COWEY, A. (1992) 'The role of the "face-cell" area in the discrimination and recognition of faces by monkeys', *Philosophical Transactions of the Royal Society of London*, B335, pp.31–8.

HINTZMAN, D.L. (1988) 'Judgements of frequency and recognition memory in a multiple-trace memory model', *Psychological Review*, 95, pp.528–51.

HUMPHREYS, G.W. (ed.) (1992) *Understanding Vision: An Interdisciplinary Perspective*, Blackwell.

HUMPHREYS, G.W. and BRUCE, V. (1989) *Visual Cognition*, Lawrence Erlbaum Associates.

HUMPHREYS, G.W. and RIDDOCH, M.J. (1987) *Visual Object Processing: A Cognitive Neuropsychological Approach*, Lawrence Erlbaum Associates.

References

HUMPHREYS, G.W., RIDDOCH, M.J. and QUINLAN, P.T. (1988) 'Cascade processes in picture identification', *Cognitive Neuropsychology*, 1900, 5(1), pp.67–103.

JACOBY, L.L. and BROOKS, L.R. (1984) 'Non-analytic cognition: memory, perception and concept learning', in Bower, G.H. (ed.) *The Psychology of Learning and Motivation: Advances in Research and Theory* (vol.18), Academic Press.

JOHNSON, M.H. and MORTON, J. (1991) *Biology and Cognitive Development: The Case of Face Recognition*, Blackwell.

JOHNSTON, R.A. and BRUCE, V. (1990) 'Lost properties? Retrieval differences between name codes and semantic codes for familiar people', *Psychological Research*, 52, pp.62–7.

JOHNSTON, R.A. and BRUCE, V. (1994) 'Who primed Roger Rabbit?', *British Journal of Psychology*, 85, pp.115–30.

JOHNSON-LAIRD, P.N. and WASON, P.C. (1977) *Thinking: Readings in Cognitive Science*, Cambridge University Press.

KEIL, F.C. (1989) *Concepts, Kinds and Cognitive Development*, MIT Press.

KOFFKA, K. (1935) *Principles of Gestalt Psychology*, Harcourt Brace Jovanovich.

KURUCZ, J. and FELDMAR, G. (1979) 'Prosopo-affective agnosia as a symptom of cerebral organic disease', *Journal of the American Geriatrics Society*, 27, pp.225–30.

KURUCZ, J., FELDMAR, G. and WERNER, W. (1979) 'Prosopo-affective agnosia associated with chronic organic brain syndrome', *Journal of the American Geriatrics Society*, 27, pp.91–5.

LABOV, W. (1973) 'The boundaries of words and their meanings', in Bailey, C.J. and Shuy, R. (eds) *New Ways of Analysing Variations in English*, Georgetown University Press.

LAKOFF, G. (1987) *Women, Fire and Dangerous Things*, Chicago University Press.

LAND, E.H. (1977) 'The retinex theory of colour vision', *Scientific American*, 237 (6), pp.108–28; 180.

MARR, D. (1976) 'Early processing of visual information', *Philosophical Transactions of the Royal Society of London*, B275, pp.483–524.

MARR, D. (1982) *Vision: A Computational Investigation into the Human Representation and Processing of Visual Information*, W.H. Freeman.

MARR, D. and HILDRETH, E. (1980) 'Theory of edge detection', *Proceedings of the Royal Society of London*, B207, pp.187–217.

MARR, D. and NISHIHARA, H.K. (1978) 'Representation and recognition of the spatial organization of three-dimensional shapes', *Proceedings of the Royal Society of London*, B200, pp.269–94.

McCLELLAND, J.L. (1981) 'Retrieving general and specific information from stored knowledge of specifics', *Proceedings of the Third Annual Meeting of the Cognitive Science Society*, pp.170–2.

McGURK, H. and MACDONALD, J. (1976) 'Hearing lips and seeing voices', *Nature*, 264, pp.746–8.

McNEILL, J.E. and WARRINGTON, E.K. (1993) 'Prosopagnosia: a face-specific disorder', *Quarterly Journal of Experimental Psychology*, 46A, pp.1–10.

MELTZOFF, A.N. and MOORE, M.K. (1977) 'Imitation of facial and manual gestures by human neonates', *Science*, 198, pp.75–8.

MERVIS, C.B. (1980) 'Category structure and the development of categorisation', in Spiro, R., Bruce, B.C. and Brewer, W.F. (eds) *Theoretical Issues in Reading Comprehension*, Lawrence Erlbaum Associates.

MERVIS, C.B., CATLIN, J. and ROSCH, E. (1976) 'Relationships among goodness-of-example, in category norms and word frequency', *Bulletin of the Psychonomic Society*, 7, pp.283–4.

MURPHY, G.L. and WRIGHT, J.C. (1984) 'Changes in conceptual structure with expertise: differences between real-world experts and novices', *Journal of Experimental Psychology: Learning Memory and Cognition*, 10(1), pp.144–55.

NEISSER, U. (ed.) (1987) *Concepts and Conceptual Development*, Cambridge University Press.

PALMER, S.E. (1992) 'Modern theories of Gestalt perception', in Humphreys, G.W. (ed.) *Understanding Vision: An Interdisciplinary Perspective*, Blackwell.

PEARSON, D.E., HANNA, E. and MARTINEZ, K. (1990) 'Computer-generated cartoons', in Barlow, H., Blakemore, C. and Weston-Smith, M. (eds) *Images and Understanding*, Cambridge University Press.

PEARSON, D.E. and ROBINSON, J.A. (1985) 'Visual communication at very low data-rates'. *Proceedings IEEE*, 73, pp.795–811.

PERRETT, D.I., HIETANEN, M.W., ORAM, M.W. and BENSON, P.J. (1992) 'Organization and functions of cells responsive to faces in the temporal cortex', *Philosophical Transactions of the Royal Society of London*, B335, pp.23–30.

PHILLIPS, R.J. (1972) 'Why are faces hard to recognise in photographic negative?', *Perception and Psychophysics*, 12, pp.425–6.

POMERANTZ, J.R. (1985) 'Perceptual organization in information processing', in Aitkenhead, A.M. and Slack, J.M. (eds) *Issues in Cognitive Modeling*, Lawrence Erlbaum Associates.

POMERANTZ, J.R. and GARNER, W.R. (1973) 'Stimulus configuration in selective attention tasks', *Perception and Psychophysics*, 14, pp.157–88.

PRICE, C.J. and HUMPHREYS, G.W. (1989) 'The effects of surface detail on object categorisation and naming', *Quarterly Journal of Experimental Psychology*, 41A, pp.797–828.

RAMACHANDRAN, V.S. (1988) 'Perception of shape from shading', *Nature*, 331, pp.133–66.

RHODES, G. (1985) 'Lateralised processes in face recognition', *British Journal of Psychology*, 76, pp.249–71.

RHODES, G., BRENNAN, S.E. and CAREY, S. (1987) 'Identification and ratings of caricatures: implications for mental representations of faces', *Cognitive Psychology*, 19, pp.473–97.

RHODES, G. and McLEAN, I.G. (1990) 'Distinctiveness and expertise effects with homogeneous stimuli: towards a model of configural coding', *Perception*, 19, pp.773–94.

ROLLS, E.T. (1992) 'Neurophysiological mechanisms underlying face processing within and beyond the temporal cortex', *Philosophical Transactions of the Royal Society of London*, B335, pp.11–21.

ROSCH, E. (1973) 'On the internal structure of perceptual and semantic categories', in Moore, T.E. (ed.) *Cognitive Development and the Acquisition of Language*, Academic Press.

References

ROSCH, E. (1975) 'Cognitive representations of semantic categories', *Journal of Experimental Psychology: General*, 104(3), pp.192–233.

ROSCH, E. and MERVIS, C.B. (1975) 'Family resemblance studies in the internal structure of categories', *Cognitive Psychology*, 7, pp.573–605.

ROSCH, E., MERVIS, C.B., GRAY, W.D., JOHNSON, D.M. and BOYES-BRAEM, P. (1976) 'Basic objects in natural categories', *Cognitive Psychology*, 8, pp.382–439.

ROTH, I.A. (ed.) (1990) *Introduction to Psychology*, Lawrence Erlbaum in association with The Open University.

RUMELHART, D.E. and NORMAN, D.A. (1985) 'Representation of knowledge', in Aitkenhead, A.M. and Slack, J.M. (eds) *Issues in Cognitive Modeling*, Lawrence Erlbaum Associates.

SERGENT, J. (1984) 'An investigation into component and configural processes underlying face recognition', *British Journal of Psychology*, 75, pp.221–42.

SMITH, E.E. and MEDIN, D.L. (1981) *Categories and Concepts*, Harvard University Press.

SUMMERFIELD, A.Q. (1979) 'Use of visual information for phonetic perception', *Phonetica*, 36, pp.314–31.

TANAKA, J.W. and FARAH, M.J. (1993) 'Parts and wholes in face recognition', *Quarterly Journal of Experimental Psychology*, 46A, pp.225–46.

THOMPSON, P. (1980) 'Margaret Thatcher — a new illusion', *Perception*, 9, pp.483–4.

VALENTINE, T. (1991) 'A unified account of the effects of distinctiveness, inversion and race in face recognition', *Quarterly Journal of Experimental Psychology*, 43A, pp.161–204.

VALENTINE, T. and BRUCE, V. (1985) 'What's up? The Margaret Thatcher illusion revisited', *Perception*, 14, pp.515–16.

VALENTINE, T. and BRUCE, V. (1986a) 'Recognising familiar faces: the role of distinctiveness and familiarity', *Canadian Journal of Psychology*, 40, pp.300–5.

VALENTINE, T. and BRUCE. V. (1986b) 'The effect of distinctiveness in recognising and classifying faces', *Perception*, 15, pp.525–35.

VALENTINE, T. and ENDO, M. (1992) 'Towards an exemplar model of face processing: the effects of race and distinctiveness', *Quarterly Journal of Experimental Psychology*, 44A, pp.671–703.

WATT, R.J. (1988) *Visual Processing: Computational, Psychophysical and Cognitive Research*, Lawrence Erlbaum Associates.

WATT, R.J. (1992) 'Faces and vision', in Bruce, V. and Burton, A.M. (eds) *Processing Images of Faces*, Ablex.

WATT, R.J. and MORGAN, M.J. (1985) 'A theory of the primitive spatial code in vision', *Vision Research*, 25, pp.1661–74.

WEISKRANTZ, L. (ed.) (1988) *Thought Without Language*, Oxford University Press.

YIN, R.K. (1969) 'Looking at upside-down faces', *Journal of Experimental Psychology*, 81, pp.141–5.

YOUNG, A.W. and ELLIS, H.D. (eds) (1989) *Handbook of Research on Face Processing*, North Holland.

YOUNG, A.W., HAY, D.C. and ELLIS, A.W. (1985) 'The faces that launched a thousand slips: everyday difficulties and errors in recognising people', *British Journal of Psychology*, 76, pp.495–523.

YOUNG, A.W., HELLAWELL, D.J. and DE HAAN, E.H.F. (1988) 'Cross-domain semantic priming in normal subjects and a prosopagnosic patient', *Quarterly Journal of Experimental Psychology*, 40A, pp.561–80.

YOUNG, A.W., HELLAWELL, D.J. and HAY, D.C. (1987) 'Configurational information in face perception', *Perception*, 16, pp.747–59.

YOUNG, A.W., McWEENY, K.H., HAY, D.C. and ELLIS, A.W. (1986a) 'Matching familiar and unfamiliar faces on identity and expression', *Psychological Research*, 48, pp.63–8.

YOUNG, A.W., McWEENY, K.H., ELLIS, A.W. and HAY, D.C. (1986b) 'Naming and categorising faces and written names', *Quarterly Journal of Experimental Psychology*, 38A, pp.297–318.

Index of Authors

Index of Authors

Hanley, J.R. and Cowell, E.S. (1988) 180

Hasselmo, M.E., Rolls, E.T. and Baylis, G.C. (1989) 170

Hay, D.C. and Young, A.W. (1982) 173, 175, 178, 181, 189

Hayes, T., Morrone, M.C. and Burr, D.C. (1986) 158

Heywood, C.A. and Cowey, A. (1992) 170

Hintzman, D.L. (1988) 47, 49

Humphreys, G.W. (ed.) (1992) 136

Humphreys, G.W. and Bruce, V. (1989) 127, 189

Humphreys, G.W. and Riddoch, M.J. (1987) 128–9

Humphreys, G.W., Riddoch, M.J. and Quinlan, P.T. (1988) 128–9, 130, 131, 133

Jacoby, L.L. and Brooks, L.R. (1984) 52–3

Johnson, M.H. and Morton, J. (1991) 190

Johnston, R.A. and Bruce, V. (1990) 176

Johnston, R.A. and Bruce, V. (1994) 192

Johnson-Laird, P.N. and Wason, P.C. (1977) 20

Keil, F.C. (1989) 69

Koffka, K. (1935) 98

Kurucz, J. and Feldmar, G. (1979) 170

Kurucz, J., Feldmar, G. and Werner, W. (1979) 170

Labov, W. (1973) 39–40

Lakoff, G. (1987) 62

Land, E.H. (1977) 76

Marr, D. (1976) 96, 104, 105

Marr, D. (1982) 82, 136

Marr, D. and Hildreth, E. (1980) 94, 95

Marr, D. and Nishihara, H.K. (1978) 108, 109, 110, 112

McClelland, J.L. (1981) 185

McGurk, H. and Macdonald, J. (1976) 171–2

McNeill, J.E. and Warrington, E.K. (1993) 191

Meltzoff, A.N. and Moore, M.K. (1977) 190

Mervis, C.B. (1980) 38

Mervis, C.B., Catlin, J. and Rosch, E. (1976) 30

Murphy, G.L. and Wright, J.C. (1984) 59

Neisser, U. (1987) 69

Palmer, S.E. (1992) 113, 155

Pearson, D.E., Hanna, E. and Martinez, K. (1990) 159

Pearson, D.E. and Robinson, J.A. (1985) 158

Perrett, D.I., Hietanen, M.W., Oram, M.W. and Benson, P.J. (1992) 170

Phillips, R.J. (1972) 157

Pomerantz, J.R. (1985) 99

Pomerantz, J.R. and Garner, W.R. (1973) 100

Price, C.J. and Humphreys, G.W. (1989) 167

Ramachandran, V.S. (1988) 158

Rhodes, G. (1985) 178

Rhodes, G., Brennan, S.E. and Carey, S. (1987) 165

Rhodes, G. and McLean, I.G. (1990) 167

Rolls, E.T. (1992) 170

Rosch, E. (1973) 31, 34–6, 37–8

Rosch, E. (1975) 31, 34–6

Rosch, E. and Mervis, C.B. (1975) 43, 44–5

Rosch, E., Mervis, C.B., Gray, W.D., Johnson, D.M. and Boyes-Braem, P. (1976) 55, 56–8

Roth, I.A. (1990) 76

Rumelhart, D.E. and Norman, D.A. (1985) 195

Sergent, J. (1984) 143, 145–7, 161

Smith, E.E. and Medin, D.L. (1981) 47, 49

Summerfield, A.Q. (1979) 169

Tanaka, J.W. and Farah, M.J. (1993) 148–51, 161

Thompson, P. (1980) 152, 153

Index of Concepts

Index of Concepts